MW00934386

THE WORKBOOK BELONGS TO:

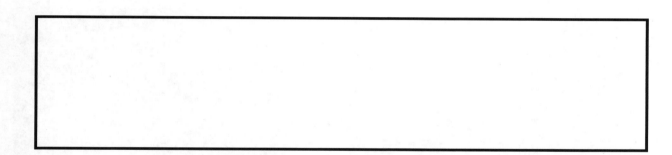

A GUIDE & WORKBOOK BY GENESIS DORSEY

BOSS BUILDER

Build Your Tribe In 30 Days

A GUIDE & WORKBOOK BY GENESIS DORSEY

BROUGHT TO YOU BY GENESISDORSEY.COM

use hashtag #bossbuilder on social media

& share a picture of you using your workbook!

COPYRIGHT, DISCLAIMER AND PERMISSION OF USE

Copyright, Disclaimer and Permission of Use

Introduction

I'm very excited about this guide and workbook. Over the next thirty days, we're going to dive deep into building your community. Many of you have watched my FREE Boss Builder training and have sent in questions regarding what you need help on. As people continue to pour in their struggle points, I wanted to choose 30 questions. I have provided answers along with questions for you to answer and action points. Now before we dive into the work, I want to tell you more about who I am and my story.

MY STORY

My business started back in 2012 with a devastating twist of events. I moved back home from Atlanta and dived into the middle of a shaky business that was being labeled as "closing in the next few weeks". Well, that didn't happen. In fact, we packed out that business with clients. That experience propelled me to become interested in business and helping others transform their dreams. I began doing graphic design and then added on web design. After that, I grew my client list and began taking note of trends and principles that appeared across the board for my clients. There are some rules that can not be changed nor reversed. When I was building my business, I didn't have much help because many people either didn't want to share information or didn't know how to help me. The void that I saw was that people needed to learn how to build their communities around their products and services. They were struggling and needed easy and applicable steps to grow. That's where I came in. Since 2016, I've transformed my business into a coaching platform where I train and lead business owners and those in ministry to build strong and highly converting communities. Are you ready to transform your business through purposeful engagement and connecting them to your "what" and "why"?

ARE YOU READY?

I'm excited. I've spread within this workbook, special teachings to keep you encouraged as well in God's Word. Let's be honest. When it comes to moving forward with your God-given vision, the road can seem tough. I've been there numerous times. Sometimes things don't look how you need them to look. However, I believe that God will never give you a vision that doesn't fill a void. We will touch on that soon within this workbook. Just know that all things are truly working together according to Romans 8:28. It's not a cliche. It's a promise. We impact the kingdom in a greater dimension when we take out the time to plant and grow communities. It's more than a product or a service that you're bringing to the marketplace. God is using you to do a great work. Keep that in mind when you feel like what you're doing isn't "good" enough. When God is involved it's always good enough. Let's jump into this work!

Outline

BUSINESS (10 DAYS)

1. What is a community when it comes to my business?
2. How do I establish my voice?
3. What is branding & how does it relate to building my tribe/community?
4. How do I tell my story and yet be transparent at the same time?
5. How do I setup & grow my email list?
6. How do I build confidence in my voice?
7. What kind of content can I create for my tribe?
8. How do I create a content calendar?
9. How can I create a funnel for my business? (Retail)
10. How can I create a funnel for my business? (Service & Sales)

SCALE & SELL (10 DAYS)

11. How do I grow my tribe when it comes to a MLM business?
12. How do I effectively price what I do?
13. How do I create product as a service-based business?
14. How can networking benefit my business? How do I do it correctly?
15. What is the purpose of a Facebook Group?
16. What is the goal of social media for my community?
17. What are Ads good for and how do I effectively use them?
18. How do I manage my time within my business to get all of this done?
19. How do you not give up when you desire to quit?
20. I own a hair salon and I need more clients. How do I gain them?

MINISTRY & CHURCH SYSTEMS (10 DAYS)

21. How do you build a community when it comes to ministry? How about within a church? Is there a difference?
22. How do we grow our church using Boss Builder strategies?
23. What tools does our church need to manage & promote our community?
24. I'm a Pastor. How do I engage our community consistently through my teachings?
25. How do we use social media to expand our reach?
26. Bonus: Facebook Basics for Churches
27. How does a church use a content calendar in planning for effective communication?
28. What should a church website include? What kind of platform should we use?
29. How can personally branding leadership help the church?
30. Bonus: Communicate Resource

SECTION ONE
BUSINESS

Question: What is a community when it comes to my business?

Your community or tribe represents the customers, followers, donors, or supporters who desire to learn more about that you do. They are not bystanders or people who randomly stop by. Your community wants to hear from you and be fed. The best example is to think of it like a town. Your business and/or ministry is a town centered on an idea or concept. It's what draws people to come and travel to hear what you have to say and provide for them.

Many times we've built products and services but we've never built a place to gather them. Many have the gift of selling but to have the gift to gather is life changing. How many times have you shared a product or service and have had to continuously chase the same people over and over again to get them to tap into what you were doing? It's frustrating and time consuming. I truly believe that for every business owner and those in ministry, capitalizing on building a community first is essential.

A community is organized to receive. Remember, that they are not scattered. They are put in place to easily obtain and apply whatever you're providing. Your community has a common goal or focus at hand. The greater you magnify that message of what you do and why you do it, your community will increase and in turn convert to profit and push that revenue number through the roof.

APPLICATION

1. Do you currently have a community? If so, provide the principles and voice that your community surrounds itself with. What is your mission statement as a business? If you do not have a community, use the space below to write out the vision and the voice that will be the foundation.

Question: How do I establish my voice?

Growing a community is also about creating and establishing your voice based upon the issue that you solve. People come because they want their problems to be solved. I want you to begin to think about what you do for the industry. Most people can never grow because they don't know what they bring to the table and how it helps people. We think that just because we sell it that people need it. However, the deeper question is this one: What issue does it solve?

If I sell lemonade from a lemonade stand, how can I make more money? Let's say there are 20 different people on the same street selling lemonade. How do I stand out? Pitch the problem and how yo solve that problem. For instance, maybe it's very hot outside. Do you know what most business owners do? Instead of talking about how their lemonade is cold and refreshing on a hot day, they simply promote that they sell lemonade. They never stand out from the crowd and scream from the mountaintops how their product or service can transform someone's day. It doesn't matter the size of what you're doing. Small things can solve a problem. Big things can solve a problem. The main thing that you need to be focused on is making sure at the end of the day, you're solving a problem and providing solutions to the market that you serve.

Now I know that the lemonade stand example was very simple but that's how simple it is. If it's too complicated to pitch how you help people solve their issues or provide them with better options, you'll always struggle to sell. Now what would make my lemonade stand expand into a larger business would be building a community around some kind of common ideal. This can stem from the vision and the mission behind your lemonade stand.

A perfect example is a lemonade stand that is all about providing organic ingredients, fun flavors, and love through impact in the community. Depending on the target audience and the branding, you can build a community around drinkers who are not just in love with lemonade but the premise of impacting those in their community and having a fresh appreciation for organic items.

APPLICATION

1. What problem do you solve? How do you solve it?

What is branding & how does it relate to building my tribe/community?

Branding is a word that has had some loose definition especially in today's market. Branding has been constrained to being how something "looks". However, it's more than that. I break it down into three areas.

1. It's what you do
2. It's what you say
3. It's what they experience

Branding is all about the experience and delivery of service. It's what makes you a "brand". Not everyone is a brand. Many are businesses and churches. What makes you a "brand" is when people can identify who you are from across the room. You brand by your actions, your words, and people's experience interacting with you.

You want your community to have an experience. In order for that to happen, it's more than just pretty pictures and beautiful displays. It's also in how you welcome them. It's in how they experience you or your services/products. The whole system that you bring them through should scream....YOU!

It includes visual identity, customer/member experience, and word of mouth!

APPLICATION

1. Now that you know what branding is, can you say that people experience "you" throughout the process you bring them through?

2. Look at your business cards, website, logo, products/services..ect. Do they look like one brand cohesively working together sharing one message? Or does it look and sound like a scattered message? (Think about your target demographic and the look that you're shooting for as a brand)

How do I tell my story and yet be transparent at the same time?

I'll respond with another question. What adds to the mission at hand? There's a difference between transparency and exposure when it comes to telling your story. You leave out the parts that don't add any value and you bring in the parts that add to the story.

Not everything that happened needs to be mentioned unless you can link the mission and purpose behind your platform to it. When I help my clients pitch their businesses, we focus on cutting down the story to the following:

1. Tell me about what led you to do what you do
2. Tell me what happened as a result
3. Tell me what life is like now

You only add in what is necessary. It has to link back to your "why" and your "what". Oversharing only happens when you don't have a strategy for what to share.

Remember that the purpose of transparency is to be open to your platform or community for the purpose of building up.

APPLICATION

1. What led you to do what you do?

2. What happened as a result?

3. What is life like now that you've started / launched / created it?

How do I setup & grow my email list?

Your email list is a great avenue for sales when it comes to your community. People really underestimate the power of email. If you're a business, people are trained by society to look for deals and get updates of their favorite brands through their email. Every week, I can expect an email from my favorite brand to tell me what's happening. Can you say the same about your business? The goal is to become a brand that they look forward to every week and will open.

Before we talk about setup, let's talk about the goal. The goal of email marketing is to create an experience and create a funnel to take a supporter from interested to paying and supporting you financially. The goal is also for them to connect with your message and become impacted by it.

For setup, here are my favorites according to your market:
1. Free: MailChimp, Mailerlite, Hubspot
2. Service-Based & Content Focused: ConvertKit, Emma
3. Retail: MailChimp, Campaign Monitor
4. All-In-One Systems (very robust): Infusionsoft, Ontraport

Now for implementation, your website will need to have some kind of sign-up box or top bar for them to join your email list. If you don't have a website yet, don't worry. If you're using any of the online software I've suggested for email marketing, they will provide you with links you can share for people to join your email list.

Depending on your website layout, you need to think about how to engage people on your site to join your list. Think about these options. Don't go overkill. Pick 2-3 from this list. No one wants to see "join, join, join, join, join, join…" plastered everywhere.

1. Bar (Sits at top of site)
2. Video with Opt-In Box
3. Slide-In Box
4. Pop-Up Box/Banner
5. Landing Page
6. In-line Box (This is a box for sign-up that sits on the page)
7. Below Blog Post Email List Box Signup
8. Sidebar (on a blog) Email Sign-Up
9. Header Design with Opt-In Box

Let's dive into how you can grow your email list. People give tons of ways for you to grow your email list. It can get pretty overwhelming. So I'm going to give you a few that are more strategic and the reasons why you should consider them.

1. Provide An Opt-In (Lead Magnet) **(Required)**
   a. The first major step is to create something that showcases what your brand is all about. This is where a free download comes in. It can be a free video course, a webinar, a worksheet, e-book,

online class, or workbook. Where most people go wrong with their opt-in is that it isn't enticing enough to draw people in AND it doesn't lead to a paid product. An opt-in is supposed to get people interested in who you are and what you provide. It's like a sampler at Costco. People love free. So once they experience your FREE, you then should have it be connected to something PAID. If you're not strategic in your opt-in, you're losing big time on introducing your paid services, programs,ect.

b. Run FB Ads with your Opt-In (**required after you have your ducks in a row**). Now to make this work well, make sure your copy (the words you use to sell what you're selling) is good. When you write your ad, put yourself in the shoes of the person who your opt-in is for. I have resources at the back of the book to help you in your FB Ad journey to collecting more leads with your ads. You also need to make sure your website/landing page is great. People run ads all day and waste their money because their brand is not ready. Make sure your funnels are setup correctly and you have a plan for conversion.

2. Provide Value & Promote the Value You're Giving **(Required)**

a. Where many people fail in email lists is that they don't give value. Your email list is so special. Make them feel like it. So many people give things away for free online all day and they never drive people to their email list. Get those that are super engaged to join your email list to get access to even more content. Setup your content calendar (See "Resource" section in the back of this guide) and work on giving your tribe an email each week with tips, tricks, and resources. Tell everyone online about how amazing that week's email is and a very short overview of what was sent out. Let the outside world feel like they are missing out and they really need to join your community. Give your email community special discounts and do special activities that only your email community gets. However, do not to forget to promote your email list. It's a constant build-up every month. It takes work but it will pay off.

3. Run Free Classes/Courses using Landing Pages

   a. This should happen continually in your business. Every 1-2 months, host FREE online special classes or webinars that help your audience. In order for them to access the class, they need to provide their email. In order to boost your list, ask your audience what they want to learn next. Research is key. Don't do what you want. Do what they want within the parameters of your skill set. Use a landing page which is a one page website they can go to. On the page include what the workshop will cover, the date, time, and instructions on how they can join in. See the back of the book for more information on Landing Pages in the resource section.

4. Cross Collaboration Online Events

   a. Now this strategy is similar to the last one except this is using the wisdom of networking. Remember that you represent one network. In order to grow your network, you need to expose yourself to other networks. How do you do that? Collaborations. You need to partner with other people who have strong engagement and bring them onto your platform. This is also how you build up credibility within your brand.

This has helped me in so many ways to build up my email list and it's what I teach my coaching clients and students. I want you to think about launching an extension of your monthly reach by hosting online interviews, special classes, and more with guest speakers, experts, ect. Invite your guest to promote on their platforms to get their network to sign up. A great way to get ahead on this is to create a short blurb for them to send to their email list as well. The strategy behind this is to think outside the box. Think about the various needs of your clients outside of your services OR think about case studies for your audience.

1. Example: I'm a fitness coach that focuses on helping mothers achieve a healthy lifestyle for themselves and their family. I collaborate with a chef to do a webinar or class on 10 Healthy Meals to Prep in under 30 Minutes. Your Upsell: Your 4 Week Fitness Program for Moms On The Go or A Meal Tracker Worksheet Pack

2. Example: I'm an author that focuses on romance novels. I collaborate with 5 couples for a special night on how to revive your love life. Those that sign-up get a free e-book called: "Spice: How to Add Flavor to Your Love Life" as well as access to the special event. Upsell: Your Most Recent Romance Book or Your Romance Box which includes your book with a few goodies for the woman in love.

3. Example: I'm a small boutique focusing on clothing for women who live busy lives but want to look awesome! I do a collaboration with a self-care expert on the importance of

self-care and taking care of your mental space. Upsell the Relaxation Special Sale which includes luxury robe, slippers, and your "Sleep Is My Cardio" t-shirt.

4. Example: I'm a women's life coach focused on helping women live boldly in their purpose through pursuing their call in ministry and entrepreneurship. I collaborate with a branding expert to teach women how to break into ministry and the marketplace with a strong online presence. I would upsell my introductory coaching program that's built for those interested in stepping into their calling. I could also upsell my latest book that's geared to women in leadership.

Other Ideas

1. Giveaways & Coupon Discounts
2. Include a link to join your email list in your email signature
3. Use a text keyword during speaking engagements or for marketing purposes for people to join via their phones.
   a. I did this for a ministry branding webinar and tons of people enjoyed signing up this way. I've put many of my clients and friends on this marketing move. Check the back of this workbook for companies that offer this.

Now guess what it's time to do? It's time to name your tribe. Not every business needs to name their tribe. It all depends on your market. For retail, many times there isn't a name for the tribe. However, if you're seeking to educate your community, naming your tribe has a big benefit. It doesn't have to be deep. However, it should scream what your mission and goal for them is all about.

APPLICATION

1. Write down some ideas for your tribe name. Ask your friends and those who understand your business if they would join your tribe. (Boss Builders is the name of my tribe. I focus on helping those in business and ministry build their communities.)

2. Come up with your tagline for your tribe. This is a very short sentence that tells them what they will learn how to do by joining your tribe.

3. Sign-Up For An Email Marketing Platform & Follow Their Setup Instructions. Write down below what you will provide on a weekly basis to your email list. Don't go overboard and over promise. If you can do one email a week, do that. Will you provide tips? Strategies?

4. Already have an email list? Pick a growth strategy and use the space below to sketch out your ideas to grow your email list.

5. What kind of opt-in will you provide? What will it be called? What will it over? (If you're in retail, please see Day #10 for help)

Question: How do I build confidence in my voice?

Many people struggle with being confident to pitch their product or service. It's really an identity issue. If you want confidence, know what you do and why you do it. When I coach business owners or those in ministry to better pitch themselves and promote their message, they usually don't really know what they are doing. I don't mean the "how". Most don't know the "what" and it isn't clear enough to form a platform on. I meet tons of people who want to encourage others. However, they don't have a clear message with a defined audience. This is why this workbook is so important because it's opening up your eyes to understand that in order to be confident you need to have a clear target to shoot at.

Another reason why people aren't confident is because they are too busy looking at everyone else and what they do and how they do it. You have to know who you're meant for and the level you're meant for. Not everyone is meant to serve experts. Some are meant to serve beginners. Some of us are meant to serve those who can afford $500 services and others are meant to serve those who can do $20K. It's all based on what you desire to focus on. Too many focus on others and then we change what we do. We change our voice. We change our purpose because we stare at somebody else and we see the huge wave of success they are having. When you stop being yourself, you'll never win being you. Why would you do that?

You have to make a decision. Leaders make decisions. Boss Builders make decisions. You must decide that you are choosing you. From there, you must realize that in order to survive in business, you must have a backbone. Business is not for those who are weak. You must strengthen your resolve. Maybe you're already in business. If you are, make your backbone stronger. Stop looking at what didn't work out last time. It will work this time if you focus and pick your target instead of trying to shoot and go with whatever sticks.

If you want to be confident, know what you do. That's it. It will clear up confusion. You won't waste your money investing in the wrong things. You won't go from one thing to another. You'll get focused and your fire will grow for what you're passionate about. You also need to realize that if God has called you to do this then you need to remove distractions and pits that you've allowed yourself to be continuously exposed to. Building something that impacts the world takes tons of energy, focus, and commitment.

Get around other confident people. Talk to yourself in the mirror and confess the Word. There aren't 100 steps to confidence.

You just need to believe in who God has made you to be. Also, realize that you can't shoot without arrows. So many are trying to serve without organizing their content, products, and services, and so you feel like no one is listening. They aren't listening because of your delivery. Thankfully, with this workbook, that will change.

APPLICATION

1. Read over this business confession that I've written for business owners

In the name of Jesus I boldly confess that I am your child and the righteousness of God. If there is anything between you & I, cover it with your blood. I thank you for giving me this dream and vision for my business. I thank you for blessing my hands so that everything I touch multiplies and produces fruit.

I plead the blood over my business. I thank you for sending me opportunities, people, and customers that will elevate my business. I thank you for giving me ideas, creative plans, and inventions that will expand my territory. I thank you for granting me influence so that I may help promote God's love in the marketplace and in arenas that need to see what true love looks like. I thank you for giving me favor with banks, merchants, suppliers, and other influencers.

I come against every attack and plan that the enemy has set forth for my business. They will not prosper! I bind up every thought in my mind that is filled with doubt and fear. I thank you for guiding me in all of my endeavors. I thank you Holy Spirit for being the voice in my head that guides me in all truth and revelation. I humble myself to be a willing and obedient vessel. Help me to help someone else today. I thank you that you are expanding my territory not just for financial growth but also to help glorify Your name in the earth!

Help me to remove all stumbling blocks and conversations that would hinder my purpose and the plans that You have for my life. I thank you for my angels that are encamped around me. I thank you that you have angels that are protecting my business and everything connected to it. Help me to guard my mind and my faith. I boldly confess that my faith is growing each and every day. I boldly confess that I am growing each and every day as a business owner and as a child of God. I boldly confess that I'm blessed coming in and I'm blessed going out. I boldly confess that my family is blessed. I thank you for protecting my family and my loved ones. I boldly confess that no matter what things may look like, I'm not going by what I see but by what God has declared to be so.

So I declare that my business is blessed. I declare that I am focused and that I have clarity in my business and in my endeavors. I declare the that blessing of the Lord makes me fruitful in all things. I declare that this will be a good day not because of what may happen but because of my obedience to God and the fact that I have expectancy in my heart that my business will flourish. I thank you God for all of these things. In Jesus Name, Amen.

What kind of content can I create for my tribe?

There is a saying that "content is king". It is true. People feed constantly off of content. What you're reading right now is content. So let's breakdown the various types of content and how to create it. I'll break it down by the platform/medium to make it easier. Remember that content is how you deliver your value to others.

1. Website
   a. Blog Posts/Articles
   b. Webinars/Videos
   c. Resources/Tools/Guides
   d. Podcast (iTunes, Soundcloud, ect.)
2. Social Media (Facebook Page, Facebook Group, Instagram, Twitter, Snapchat, Periscope, YouTube, Pinterest, ect.)
   a. Text Posts with Tips/Encouragement/Strategies
   b. Video Posts with Tips/Encouragement/Strategies
   c. Photo/Graphic Posts with Tips/Encouragement/Strategies
   d. Live Videos with Strategic Goals for Community & Help
3. Email Marketing
   a. Email with alert of new blog post on the site
   b. Email containing Tips/Encouragement/Strategies
4. In-Person
   a. Live Keynote
   b. Panel/Workshop
   c. Vendor/Exhibitor Table providing resources/guides

APPLICATION

1. What kind of content can you promise to deliver monthly? How often? Write it all out below. Remember, don't start out over-promising.

2. It's time to begin getting serious about coming out strong. I want you to look at the calendar and figure out when you will launch your content campaign. In other words, this is when you'll begin to rollout monthly content on your platforms. What month will you begin?

How do I create a content calendar?

Now that you've laid out what content you will produce, now it's time to create a schedule for your content. In my office, I sketch mine out on a large dry erase board for ideas. From there I type everything in a Google Doc that is edited every month.

I've attached in the back of this workbook sheets for you to plan out your content calendar. I'll use this time to tell you the things you need to consider in your content calendar.

First, you need to pick the platforms that you will hit on. You can't be on every social media platform. Unless you have hired someone to run your social media platforms for you on a daily basis, you need to think smart. Pick 3 platforms you can nail down every week outside of your email list as a platform. Mine are my email list, Instagram and Facebook. I dabble in YouTube and Twitter from time to time but I've been extremely consistent in the first three.

Second, you want to gather pick a theme for the month. This is the easiest way to organize content in my opinion. If you want to jump ahead, pick 12 topics you want to cover for the next 12 months. By doing that, you can organize a whole year ahead of time. Once you pick a theme for that month, divide it into 4 weeks. If a month has 5 weeks, use the last month to do a special wrap-up of the whole month via a live video or an email to your tribe.

Third, go into a Google Doc and break down the four weeks into sub-topics. Below is an example for a DIY Website Expert who wants to teach their tribe how to create landing pages. This month they want to focus on selling their Landing Page Template Kit.

Theme for January (insert year): How to Create A Landing Page

Week One: Create Your Offer
Week Two: Write Your Copy
Week Three: Layout Your Page
Week Four: Launch & Collect Leads

Now, remember I had you list the kind of content you would provide and how often? So what you will do next is under each week, you'll list what you will post to each platform.

Why? Do you know how many business owners who treat their platforms like last minute projects? They force themselves to think of good quotes the day of and stress out when they forget to post. By creating a content calendar, you'll have every month planned in advance and you'll be more confident of what you're introducing to your community. You'll also be confident of what you're selling because the entire month will help you promote a chosen service/product that you offer.

APPLICATION

1. Fill out the information below.

A. What will be the main topic/theme for the first month?

*   Week 1 Topic:

*   Week 2 Topic:

*   Week 3 Topic:

*   Week 4 Topic:

Now go to the back of the workbook and access your content calendar to begin planning your content monthly.

How can I create a funnel for my business in retail?

Funnels are essential in business. Every interested person is a lead. You want to turn a lead into a customer. Here is my easy breakdown for creating leads in retail. This is for those that are focused on commerce based business for products.

1. Promote Your Opt-In: In retail, this is usually a coupon code or promotion that they access by providing their email address. If you want to be really strategic, let the opt-in be something that is more of a guide. Maybe it's a guide or a checklist on how to use your most popular product or how to rock a simple statement piece. Maybe it's a crash course guide on how why they need your product and how it can help them do (fill in the blank). Think about their end goals as the shopper. When they purchase your product what are they really wanting as the result?

2. Once they sign-up, build out a campaign that is sent to them over the next few days as "onboarding".
    - Sending Course for 3 Days?
        - Day 1-3 = course
        - Day 4 = Upsell a special offer
    - Sending a coupon?
        - Day 1 = coupon/discount
        - Day 2 = Welcome email to community/store/family

- Wait a few days (3-5 days)
- Send another email with a video/link to show them more information about your product and include some demonstration. Clothing? Do a demo video on how to rock a popular item in your store within an outfit. Tool? Do a demo video showing how to use it. Software? Share a demo video on how it will help them reach their goals faster. If you don't want to do a video, do a blog post instead that you share with your new subscriber.

Now the great thing about retail is that your on-boarding doesn't have to drag out like someone in a service-based business. Businesses in retail send emails almost daily to shoppers. I suggest sending out regular emails for retail 2-3 times a week to get your subscribers taking you seriously as a store.

If you're in retail, you must send out emails on the weekend. Friday is when the majority of shoppers get paid. Every Friday, consumers should see an email in their inbox. This is a requirement. If you slack on sending emails on the weekend, you will lose on sales. When you drop collections or retail products, days matter. The same goes for Holidays. Make sure you take advantage of holidays, especially the winter season. This is why having that content calendar and plan ahead of time is essential so that you can prep your emails and campaigns. Also, switch up your opt-in every 3-5 months to keep it fresh. During the Holiday Season, provide a seasonal code like "winter10" to offer 10% off during the winter by signing up.

APPLICATION

1. Below, sketch out your funnel process from opt-in to email. What is your opt-in? What emails will be sent via your funnel to promote community and conversion?

How can I create a funnel for my business in service-based?

Service based businesses create funnels for a lead cycle. You're going to follow the similar model of the retail funnel but a sales funnel is usually laid out longer. For many in the service-based business industry, the investment of the consumer is larger. Therefore, there is some convincing and trust that needs to happen and be built up. Let's sketch out the funnel for my business that's a basic layout.

Boss Builder Funnel

1. Landing Page Explaining Boss Builder Free 2-Day Training
2. Lead signs-up and receives welcome email where I explain why the training is so important
3. Email sent with links to Boss Builder Free 2-Day Training to watch. I let them know what each day covers.
   a. The Boss Builder Training is pre-recorded. I'm not going live every single time someone signs up. I uploaded them into YouTube as "unlisted" (privacy setting) and share the links.
4. After 24 Hours, Boss Builder Workbook up-sell Sent for $24.99
5. I then re-target those who have purchased the book, for Boss Builder 4 Week Training Course for $197.
   a. The Boss Builder 4 Week Training is pre-recorded content with downloads already designed. Evergreen programs/ courses are pre-recorded content that can be sold while you

sleep. These are self-paced courses/classes that you create once and you can market and promote for people to enroll.

Remember that those in the Boss Builder funnel, will receive regular emails every week with tips & tricks from me. A funnel is a designated journey a lead takes with a focus for a sale. Once they provide their email for the training, they are now on my email list until they unsubscribe. Don't go overboard with the on-boarding. Let your subscribers breathe.

Coaching Funnel
1. Promotion of Coaching Programs with Free Webinars
2. Lead Watches Webinar/Training where I up-sell at the end with a chance for them to sit down with me for a call for them to begin living their dreams by building their communities
3. Lead signs-up for a Discovery Session for 15 Minutes
    a. Discovery Session is not a coaching session. It's for them to tell me their goals and desires. It's a sales call.
    b. I use a scheduling system via a link. You want to keep this process automated. No one should be emailing you to schedule a call. Use a booking form so that people can book without needing you to do so.
4. Discovery Session Call with a goal to sell a coaching program
5. If yes, I sign them up for a coaching program. If no, I re-target them down the road and offer a "check-in" call. Remember, that there is money in the follow-up. Keeping in touch with those interested down the road can lead to more clients. Some clients just need to save up.

APPLICATION

1. Below, sketch out your funnel process from opt-in to email. What is your opt-in? What emails will be sent via your funnel to promote community and conversion? What will be your up-sell? Are you offering a program or a larger service for them to try?

SECTION TWO
SCALE & SELL

How do I grow my tribe when it comes to a MLM business?

Multi-Level Marketing was something that at first I was extremely against. However, over time, I saw a void within this sector of sales. Distributors did not know how to gather and sell. I would see people post daily about products and more. The fact is that you make more money adding people under your team versus selling product. The goal for distributors is to rise in the ranks of their company.

How do you grow your distribution team? Community. What most distributors miss is that they are so focused on people joining that they haven't presented a picture that will draw people. What I teach every week online and in-person can be applied to those in the MLM world. Why? Because community is at the heart of everything.

What I see is that many in MLM join "coaching groups" and the ones who receive the large checks and the new ranks are those who have started a movement via community. When I coach MLM distributors the first thing that we focus on is the community. This is before the sales, inviting them to parties,ect.

What will draw people to join your own tribe within the company? It's more than just making money. People are draw to a lifestyle. For some, it's about being a young millennial that's glamorous and the income made through sales achieve that.

For others, it's the healthy lifestyle movement or the financial building lifestyle. You have to target just like it was your own business and you were the CEO or owner. What are the common cores of your community? What do you all desire to do? What's your "why"? What age/gender are you targeting? What is the name of your tribe?

For some it's a name of a tribe or a slogan. Many in the MLM community have done both and have excelled. If you're interested in joining a MLM, the greatest thing you can do is to create a branded experience for your community. Make them feel as if they are apart of something exclusive. For some it's about making more money. However, what does money bring? There are people who are already making money. You'll have to give them something greater than just the ability to make money. Can I provide for you further information about community within a MLM?

Many times on social media, I see people who ask me if I would like to make an additional $500 to $750 a month in the holiday season or anytime in general. Now many people will say "yes" and might sign up. However, guess what happens? You have low retention. So you drew them to make more money but unless they are Type-A, which most people aren't, they will fall off. You need a deeper reason.

APPLICATION

If you haven't already, go back through section one and fill out the questions on community and building your tribe.

1. What types of products/services do you sell? What is their purpose?

2. What is the name of your tribe? Do you have a slogan for what your tribe does? Think about the "one thing" that we talked about in the first section.

3. After reading today's breakdown, what could you do differently to create a movement to bring in other distributors? Think about all the previous days where Genesis broke down community building. What techniques from MLM, that you've learned, can you infuse with what Genesis has taught?

Boss Builder: Scale & Sell

How do I effectively price what I do?

This is one of the top five questions that I get. However, you may not like what I have to say. Your price is based upon many factors. However, it's not that complicated. Here are some starting factors that come into play with price.

Starting Factors
- Your Target Demographic
- The Market Price Average
- Your skill-set & experience
- The experience that you will give your customers

When I first got started in graphic design, I made some major mistakes. However, there are some things that you truly learn along the way. Experience is not the best teacher but in being an entrepreneur, it will teach you like you've never wanted to be taught before. Believe me. Nevertheless, when I first got started, I charged $50 for logos and $150 for websites. Let me tell you why.

For starters, the only example I had when starting was the internet including social media. I did not look at the industry average nor the price point I needed to sell at to generate the proper revenue. You can't get into business just slapping prices onto the wall and hoping that something sticks. That's what most business owners do. They don't study the market nor do they analyze what they need to generate. What most inexperienced entrepreneurs do is change their prices according to non-valuing customers. What do I mean by this?

- Potential Customer (non-valuing): How much do you charge for this service?
- Owner: States price (true price)
- Potential Customer: Well, I've been quoted (quotes an extremely low price).
- Owner: Well I can do that! (Now panicking)

This is why I see people struggling day in and day out with their business. I can't tell you what to charge. This is why you need a mentor in your market who can help guide you. God will provide for you someone who can give you wisdom and knowledge. It may not be a direct mentor. It can be an indirect mentor which means you follow them from far away and listen to their instruction. Don't follow the gurus who don't have any credibility. Research their companies and see what people say. Also, hear for their heart and not their marketing lingo. When people wish for you to win, they won't sell you horrible gimmicks. They won't use your lack of wisdom to their benefit. They will see your lack of wisdom and show you what you're missing. Lastly, I can't say this again and again but please study the market and gain experience. Get an internship. Sign up for programs near you that will help further you in your skills. By being around different agencies, owners, business, and more, you will learn how the business works. When you ignore following those who have gone before you, you will always charge below your worth.

APPLICATION

1. If you've been struggling to establish your pricing, why is that? How will you get over it and what will you do so that you won't shrink back?

2. How do you base your pricing, programs, and ect.?

3. List some things you can do in the next 30 days, 60 days, and 90 days that will help you better understand your field in business

How do I create product as a service-based business?

Product development is on the rise especially within service-based businesses. The biggest way to diversify your money is to offer different types of products. I want to provide for you a quick list of the types of things your business can sell to position yourself for another stream of revenue.

- Books and Digital Books (E-Books, Workbooks, Guides)
- Audio Downloads & Audio Courses
- Online Course & Webinars (Online School)
- Apparel (T-Shirts, Wall artwork, Mugs, ect.)

Now the thing about producing product is that you need to understand release times and the structure for distribution. The worst thing you can do is create a product at the wrong time and in the wrong season. Products also must fill a void. I'm sure there are some things that you want to produce but if it's something you want but nobody else wants, produce one copy just for you to keep. Just don't put it out for sale. It reminds me of when I started to dive into drop shipping apparel. There were some apparel designs that I only liked. I wanted to wear them. However, they weren't for the masses. So I got one shirt printed and placed it in my closet. I didn't put it up for sale.

You can't get mad when you only produce what you want and no one else buys and you don't have any sales. Give the people what they want. Now let's get back to the season and timing. You build up product releases. You don't just drop product.

Now my favorite thing to talk about when it comes to planning the release of a project is to get ready for "the drop". This is where you either are an expert or a complete failure. If you are a complete failure don't worry. You'll work up to being an expert. "The drop" will teach you extreme patience. Think of it like leaks. Whether you agree with her life or not, Beyonce understands the power of "the drop". Dropping hints here and there and telling people that something amazing is coming to help them (fill in the blank) builds up hype. As you build up the hype, make sure they are on your email list so that they can be prepared for whatever you're releasing.

Now you can either gather the people in your main email list or you can create another list as the "waiting list" where people can add their name and email so that they are the first to be able to order when you open up "the doors" for people to sign up or purchase. It's completely up to you whatever method you use. However, build the hype up. Whenever you release something, don't just drop it in front of people's faces and expect them to be excited. There's a 50/50 percent chance that they will run to you supporting or they will walk far away. People want to join in with you in the celebration. I've learned that involving people in the release makes them feel apart of the movement. They feel like they were with you in the trenches with you. Remember, you're building community. It's like a continual Christmas for your audience. The greatest thing about Christmas is that there is a build-up. There is an entire campaign around the promotion of Christmas. Remember the 12 Days of Christmas? The entire song is about a build-up. Each day there is a gift. Well apply that to your business.

Remember when we discussed having a content calendar? Having a content calendar along with your sales goals for the entire year helps you set a flow for your business. Think about it. If you know what you're going to focus on during your second quarter of your business, you should have products lined up to match with whatever you will be presenting to your customer base. Do you have a plan for your product releases this year or more specifically this upcoming month? If not, you need to have a plan and I suggest you get it in motion as soon as possible. Remember that your sales goals must be hit. Another note that must be added is that whenever you get on a "live", do a webinar, do a talk, or provide tips, give people somewhere to go. In order to have sales, you must push the product. Don't just create it and announce it once. Continuously put it in your customer's faces over and over again. How often? I suggest at least 2-3 times a week. Focus though on a product.

When you're in a service based business, remember that you're already promoting your consistent services that you offer through the year. So pick moments during the month when you focus on the product that matches the content that you're pushing out at that time.

APPLICATION

1. What products will you develop in the next 3-6 months? Write down based upon your content calendar and the input of your community, what you need to create. You can put out a poll to gather what people want to get from you.

2. What will be your product release plan? Develop your plan below for your next product release.

How can networking benefit my business? How do I do it correctly?

Networking is key to your business. It's all about building up your circle of relationships that will benefit your life personally and professionally. You want to make sure you have a strong circle around you. Networking accomplishes that. The real question is how and who do I network with. The purpose of networking is to literally create a "net". The types of events you go to are key because of the quality of people that are there. When I go to events, I break them into two categories. Some events are events where the purpose is to not meet connections but to meet my community. There are some events where there will not be one soul who can help elevate your business. However, you might meet 1,000 new customers. Knowing what type of event you're going to will help you better present yourself. I present myself differently to my community members than I do someone who may be able to help me scale my business.

Of course the premise of the conversation is the same at first. You introduce yourself and who you are. From there, the conversation must be natural to flow. The worst thing you can do is force a conversation. Genuine conversations are the most beneficial because the people who will later connect with you are truly there to benefit and help you. Not everyone is here in this world to help you. It's best you understand that now. Not every networking event is truly a networking event. Some events are nothing but dating and adultery funded events where the soul purpose is to work the flesh instead of creating beneficial partnerships.

Also, get out of your area of where you live. Many times people network within the same area. While you want to establish connections locally, make it an effort to go out of town once a month to a major networking event. You want to build global partnerships. Notice, I didn't say nationally. Think bigger. Many times, you never know what you will need until you need it. So setup connections now so that if and when you need something, you have people within your contact list that you can reach out to.

Now one of the main issues for many people when it comes to networking is that they think that you meet someone once and that's it. You know the drill. Talk. Provide the business card. Follow-up but not as strong as it should be. You forget them and they forget you. It's a relationship. You have to work those relationships. I don't understand how people get into business and want to stay on this island. You never do business lunches. You don't send emails to check in on your networking relationships. You don't send Holiday gifts to particular people. You never follow-up with a professional email to re-establish the connection. However, you want to rule the marketplace. Change how you interact with people. You need to interact with diversity as well. Go past your socio-economic level. Get outside your race. Get outside your area. Build a diverse network and watch your reach expand including your influence.

APPLICATION

1. When it comes to networking, what are your biggest fears or struggles? Why do you think that is? How will you change that?

2. What events will you be going to in the next month? How about larger conferences, summits, and events that you can attend in the next 3-6 months? Maybe even the next year?

3. Practice in the mirror or with some friends working a crowd. "Working a crowd" simply means being able to flow through a crowd and establishing connections and partnerships. Many times people simply stand in a corner and just wait for people to walk up to them. Change that. You don't need to hand your business card to everyone. However, maybe it's connecting on social media. Do have a clear delivery on what you do? Go back to the first section to make sure there is clarity in your presentation. Can you deliver your purpose within one sentence as an opener? If not, make changes so that you can network with ease.

What is the purpose of a Facebook Group?

So many people miss the purpose of a Facebook Group. I know this because people continuously add me to their groups in hope that I will support them or buy from them. Every Facebook Group needs a purpose. Some groups are not meant for business. Some are meant for trivial pleasure where people gather as a community around a common object, theme, purpose, or intent.

Now in business, you need an end goal. Not every group is meant to be some serious business group. You can make a group fun. It just needs to have a funnel so that as people come in, you're benefitting from their participation. This is why it's important that you have an email marketing platform so that as people come in, they can get some kind of relating freebie that will cause them to become potential customers. I saw a group blow up almost overnight with a focus on men with beards. Women joined the group looking to see men with beards and men joined to see the women that enjoyed the beards. The group grew like wildfire. The next move? Well the owner had a beard grooming brand. However, the group blew up because of the people joining who loved the beards. Who was the true customer? When you don't have any strategy, a good idea can become a burdensome one because you need to convert that growth to money.

You have to look at who your group will attract and if you can create products to further propel that love and community feeling. Going back to our product development section, we talked about the several things you can create and sell. Have a plan. You also need to have order. Groups must have rules. Why? Because without order, a mess will be created. People are people which means they are prone to creating negative events if they are allowed. People will try it. Don't give them an open door. As your group grows, get moderators and admins who can engage, protect, and monitor the group.

Now some groups are meant to be resource-based groups. These are groups where the community comes together to help others achieve a similar goal. Allowing your community members to come in and ask questions and get help are forms of content. However, in those types of groups, make sure you maintain your voice and visibility. There are people who will come in and they may have more accolades or fame than you. However, you're the creator of the group. I'm not saying flex yourself. What I mean is that post branded content connected to the group. Do your own "lives" as the creator to make sure that there is a main voice guiding the group. This is very important. Yes, it's a community. Yes, it's about people enjoying themselves and gaining a sense of pride around a common focus. However, you're who started the group. Don't forget that.

As the creator of the group, present fun ways people can engage. With the "live streaming" feature, this presents so many opportunities for your community to become engaged with a group. Create specific days to where approved community members can provide content. People want to put themselves on. That is human nature. Use it to your benefit and let the community provide content. So many creators drain themselves trying to be the sole creator of the content. Why would I do that when the content could be largely provided by the community themselves? In the beard group, the community was provided with content from the community members. The last thing is that make sure you have time to support and push the FB group. Because they are so many groups, you need to make sure your group won't be "another group". You don't have to rack your brain trying to reinvent the wheel. However, be original in the sense of your purpose and don't try to compete with another group. Also, pray that God sends you the right help to grow the group.

APPLICATION

1. What's the purpose of your group? What do you seek to do and how will you do it?

2. How will this community connect to your business or to a new one?

3. Will this be built on community based content or will it also include content from you?

What is the goal of social media for my community?

Social media serves an instrumental purpose, especially in this digital age. Social media is a funnel for your community. Remember that it's not an end point. It's a platform where you can express your goal, you purpose, and your products/services. You need to have a purpose within your social media world. Because this a broad question, we're going to look at this from a general scope.

Social media helps you connect with your potential and current community base. You must pick 2-3 platforms (in the beginning) that you can focus on. I really only suggest that number when you're beginning because you have to build up consistency. You can have a desire to be everywhere but it's better to be where you can serve well. I suggest Facebook and Instagram as the two main platforms. You can either do both or pick one along with others such as Snapchat, Pinterest, YouTube, Periscope, and other platforms to support the brand socially.

Engagement is within the goal of creating a funnel. You need to get people talking, tagging others, and gaining interest to then make a purchase. You can have tons of followers but if you don't have engagement and people aren't talking, it means nothing. If you only have 100 followers and 50 of them are talking and engaging on a consistent basis, you have a 50% engagement factor. Do you know how big that is? Most only have between 10-20% when it comes to engagement when it comes to the ratio of your total followers to the number of people liking and commenting.

Showing up is a requirement on social media. Give the people what they want. Also, make sure what you post and share aligns to your brand. You want people to come to your profile and know it's you. The worst thing you can do is have all of your social media platforms look like three different businesses. Keep the colors and fonts and look the same across the board.

With live streaming, business owners are also getting the chance to provide behind the scenes access to their community. Your team can stream live showing them the preparation for a collection or a product drop. You can share tips and advice. Remember, have these scheduled and planned in your content calendar. You should have a social media calendar where you can plan out when you will post and the content you will post. In the back of this guide, there is a template you can follow. If I could provide any more general advice, I would say that automation is your friend. Use automation to post and as you grow and then get back on the platforms during the day to check in and respond to comments and questions. For many businesses, social media is turning into a form of customer service. Customers and potential clients are asking questions about shipping times, delivery of product, cost, contact info, and much more. Don't miss out on potential sales.

APPLICATION

1. What platforms are you consistent on? What platforms will you work on to be more consistent on? How will you become more consistency? What will change this time?

2. How will you increase engagement and how will you convert that engagement to sales?

What are Ads good for and how do I effectively use them?

Facebook Ads confuse many business owners. It's not made nor created for you to just go in and win. For Facebook this is a business. If you don't know what you're doing, you will waste money. Plain and simple. I'm not a Facebook Ad expert so I'm going to answer this from the scope of how Facebook Ads connect to community and the purpose. Before you go into doing Facebook Ads, you have to know a very important factor. What's the purpose and where do you want them to go after they click or connect?

People assume that if they put up an ad that they will blow up overnight. If you've done ads before you'll know how hilarious this previous sentence is because it rarely happens unless it's just your special day and you become a blow-up sensation overnight. Those are rare cases and I'm not going to push you on based upon rare cases. With Facebook Ads, there are so many different purposes. The majority of Facebook Ads are broken down into the following:

- "Get this FREE (download, e-book, worksheet)
- "Watch this FREE (webinar, conference,ect.)
- "Get 10% off (coupon, special code, offer,ect.)
- Click Bait (click this to see how so & so became a celebrity)
  - Gossip column/article, cheesy story

You should know that when you're doing Ads, you want to capture the lead. So they need to sign up, use the coupon, or download so that in exchange you get something. You can't spend money and not have a funnel for what happens once they click. If you're giving away a free download or video, you need to setup a landing page. Many people use Leadpages or Clickfunnels to set these up. You can also use Unbound or larger platforms like Ontraport or ConvertKit to build these out. Some of the email marketing platforms that I've suggested in previous days have landing pages as apart of the package.

The biggest thing that most people don't do when creating Ads is to test your ads. You don't just run them. You test them. When I first began ads, I only did one. However, you need to do at least three ads to test and put a $5 budget on each for about 7-14 days to see which one performs best. Whichever one runs best, that's the one you put more money into. You want to test copy (the words that goes with the video/photo) and you want to test the images as well as the video that's being used. There are many factors that make up a good ad. Keep that in mind. Facebook (they own Instagram) has online courses and bootcamps you can sign up for to learn how to better use Ads for your business. I highly suggest that you watch them. The worst thing you can do is throw money at something you have no idea about. At the back of the book are resources including their resources for you to use at your disposal. There also ads for other platforms such as Google, Pinterest, and Twitter. Again, you need to research and study. If you don't know what to do, then hire someone who does.

APPLICATION

1. What would you do an ad for? What is the product or service that needs the ad?

2. What is the demographic that you will focus on to pitch to them the item?

3. Do you need to setup a landing page or will it take them to the website of purchase? If so, what does it need to include? What will the coupon be for and how much?

4. Do you know what a Facebook Pixel is and do you have it installed on your website?

5. Have you watched Facebook's courses on Facebook Ads? If so, what changes do you need to make to your ads to increase results? Write them down below for future notes. (If not, check the resource area in the back of this guide)

How do I manage my time within my business to get all of this done?

Time management is key in the business world. You must learn how to manage. Many are looking for balance in their business. Balance is relative. It looks different to every person. Remember that God is the one who brings true balance. He is the one who makes it all work together. There are some natural and spiritual keys that I want to provide for getting it all done.

Automation and systems are your friend in business. You have to learn what you need to do physically and what a system or technology can do for you. Let me fill you in on my system when it comes to keeping it all together.

- Social Media (Automate Posts being posted by using Buffer & Grum for Instagram, Facebook, and Twitter)
- Squarespace (Website Platform) with Acuity (For Booking Coaching Calls & Live Classes, and Programs) and Mailchimp w/ Privy Plugin (Email Funnel for Boss Builder)
- Hubspot Marketing (for large sales calls & targeting leads)
- Glip for clients to submit documents for coaching program and for us to go back on forth on finalizing projects
- PayPal and Stripe for payment systems to take payments (I use Jotform for forms to collect special payment and so forth)
- Thinkific for online courses (Evergreen coaching courses) where people can sign up and work on their own pace

I use technology heavily because in order to scale you can't do it all. I also hire. If you don't hire, you will expire. You will not be able to produce in the form in which you need to. Many entrepreneurs don't think they have the money to hire. You don't have to hire full time. It can be a contract position or a part-time position. You also can hire accountants, lawyers, contractors, and more to get the job done! However, in your business goals for each quarter, you need to know how much money you need to bring in to hire.

The reason why the majority of entrepreneurs burn out is because they are not organized. Organization brings freedom. Not your ideas. You can execute and be a mess. If we would be honest, you won't be an expert executioner for too long. You will soon give up. Why? Because success has to be managed. It has to be focused and intentional. You can't be intentional in the midst of chaos. Organize your receipts. Implement a system. Use technology to remove the daily headaches of doing the simple things.

It's better to reduce your salary to something extremely low as the owner so that you can afford to bring in employees who can bring in more sales. You have to think long term. Too many think short term and burn themselves out. Here are some other things you need to take into consideration.
- Take vacations or just get out of town (1-3 hours away)
- Sleep (get your 6 hours of sleep minimum)
- Workout (no matter your size)
- Drink water (Juice is not water. Drink water.)

APPLICATION

1. Would you say that you have allowed God to be your balance? If not, why not? What have you been trying to do without His grace?

2. Write down your systems within your business. What areas do you need to bring a system into? Is the system streamlined? In other words,

How do you not give up when you desire to quit?

The average quit time is 2-3 years for business owners. So many people get started and stop. The exciting part is announcing that you've launched. After that, the work comes into play. It's the work that proves whether or not what you're doing is what you should be doing. Are you called to this? Or are you doing something that you just want to pick up to make some money?

This is why in the first section of this workbook, we dived into your "why". Most people give up because they forgot why they got started. Here are some things you can do so that you won't give up.
- Know Your "Why"
- Remove distractions
- Check your circle
- Keep your faith in line with the Word
- Surround yourself with the Word

The truth of the matter is that we give up when we lose sight of what's ahead. Entrepreneurship is not for the faint of heart. It's for those who have faith in what they are doing. You have to have a deeper purpose or you will be swept by surface situations. God would never birth something within you and not give you the ability to raise it. that's why you have to be called and assigned. You can't flow in what God has not assigned you with. God has called women to be mothers and not fathers. Why? Well we know this because women are equipped to birth children which makes them mothers. They have been equipped with the right tools and the mindset to handle what they will soon face. This is why you can't just pick up a business and then ask God to equip you for it.

If you're quitting, you need to get your sight back. Business is too volatile to base things off of how it looks at the time. You have to base things off of what God says. I'm not negating the knowledge that you must have in order to operate business. All that I'm saying is don't allow your knowledge to replace your faith. Instead, it should equip your faith to now have a target of belief. What were you focusing on that took your eyes off of the promise?

We see this happen with Sarah, the wife of Abraham. She took her eyes off of what God promised and suggested to Abram that he lay down with Hagar. Ishmael was born but he was not the promise. We see this happen with Saul. Saul was supposed to wait on Samuel and because of his lack of patience. He ends up losing his crown. What have you focused on that is causing you to birth distractions instead of destiny? If God has blessed you and assigned you to be within the marketplace, you need to hold on to that. When you let go, you're letting go of purpose. Sometimes we have too much faith in what we can see when faith is relying upon what you can't see. It's having so much trust that God's Word is truth instead of your experiences. At all times, trust God. He will do exactly what He promised. You just need to believe it and not let go. If you let it go, it's time to get it back.

APPLICATION

1. In this season in your life, would you say that you're focused on the promise or more on the situation? What does your faith need right now in order for you to fulfill your next assignment?

2. Why is your role as an entrepreneur deeper than something natural? What is the spiritual component to being an entrepreneur?

3. How are you going to keep your joy when it comes to your calling? What will you do to protect your love for your business?

I own a hair salon and I need more clients. How do I gain them?

This is a very layered question but many of the things that I discussed in the first section are vital to the success of a hair salon or even as a stylist. What's your "one thing"? What do you do well as a salon? You build up on that one thing and still perform additional services. What do you want to be known for? Saying that you want to be a great salon is not enough. People have several options for where they go. Pick a focus and go extremely hard on that focus to make yourself and your salon an expert.

Local word of mouth is essential which means you must have good visibility. When you meet people, make sure you leave a great impression. It's about creating relationships for a lifetime goal to help them have amazing hair experiences. Positioning yourself as an expert in business and hair is a great way to align your salon with excellence. Think about local or regional / national hair shows where you're not just an exhibitor or vendor but also an expert. Host local events with the community to position yourself as apart of the area your business is located in. Everywhere you go, you should be a walking billboard for your business. Think about having business cards on hand where they can go to your website to schedule appointments with ease.

Do not use social media as a billboard where you slap up pictures and tell people to come. That's not how you create urgency nor desire. You need to become an expert. Share tips and insight on how people can better take care of their hair. Discuss how coming to your salon will change their life. Don't just give help. Connect it back to the salon so that they feel as if they must come to you to experience the fullness of your wisdom and help.

One of the biggest issues I've seen is that people are very talented but they look like something blown from the wind. You are your brand and that means that presentation is everything. This also goes for your staff. Everyone should have some form of dress code and "look" that represents your salon. You should also have systems in place for retaining customers. As a business coach that has worked with several salons, most don't use sufficient systems that streamline the customer experience.

Your staff is everything when it comes to the success of your business. Train them to be you. They should understand the company culture, values, and the vision. Whoever you hire that is going against that must be fired, no exceptions. You grow your salon by hiring great people. In the hair industry, hiring great salon stylists can be a huge plus. However, study your industry to learn how to keep them on board. Retention of stylists is something many salons struggle with because they don't treat their stylists as true employees with company culture. Create a workplace where people love to come.

I can't say this enough but staff meetings and trainings are essential. As people change so should your salon to adapt to their needs. If certain trends are coming into people's worlds, your salon should know how to embrace those trends and infuse them into your offerings. Also, discuss monthly goals for your salon and targets that you want to hit as an entire team. Now in order to do this, you need to know your back-end as the owner.

Think about this process. A customer walks in and is scheduled with a stylist. The stylist performs the service and payment is received. The customer leaves. What technology is tracking that? Are you sending out reminder emails to alert clients of upcoming appointments? As a business owner, you should be able to know how many customers have walked into your door, the average customer spend, and how many up-sells happened (upgrades, salon products sold,ect.). You should know all of this without going through stacks of paperwork or receipts. Use technology to your advantage. I highly suggest attending conferences and expos for salon owners and those in the hair industry so that you aren't struggling on purpose.

The data never lies. It will show you where the holes are in sales and what your customers are continuously coming back for and who they are coming back for. Use Holiday Seasons and other special times of the year to offer special blowout sales to boost customers coming into the door and offer your most popular services. In short, have a streamlined system, become known as an expert, and make sure your salon stands out for something.

APPLICATION

1. What does your salon specialize in? How have you as the owner worked to connect your expertise to the success of the salon?

2. Do you currently have staff? How can you improve your monthly team meetings to shift your staff to move towards the future of hair care?

3. What technology do you use to streamline the customer experience? What is your strategy for them coming back? How often do you engage with your customer after they've had an experience at your salon?

SECTION THREE

MINISTRY & CHURCH SYSTEMS

How do you build a community when it comes to ministry? How about within a church? Is there a difference?

Community building with a ministry versus a church are similar but there are definitely major distinctions. Let's tackle them as one and then individually so that we can best fit the needs of what you're looking to accomplish.

When it comes to ministry overall, it works very much like what we covered in the first section. God gives every ministry a unique purpose. There should be a particular group of people you seek to reach and a unique way you connect with them. For every spiritual leader, God always plants a vision of what they are to accomplish in the earth. You can not build community without a clear vision for what you seek to do and how you will do it. People unite around clear missions and goals. When it comes to building a community in ministry, your main goal should be presenting a clear objective and staying focused on that objective.

I launched a women's ministry back in 2012 using YouTube. I did live teachings via Google Hangout and had no idea how to build a community. I just knew that God gave me a mission. One of the most critical words of advice I can give a ministry that is not a church is to have a system to gather those that are interested in what you do. If you go back to some of the previous days, I discussed email marketing and having a website. These two items are very important.

Have the gift to gather and the gift to impart. Using email marketing to alert those who are connected to your ministry is an amazing way to bring value. When I finally understood the power of using social media to push people to the website and the email list, we were able to really build something monumental. We were able to gather data on who our community consisted of, where they lived, phone numbers, and so much more.

On our website, we offered an opt-in. It was our downloadable bible studies that now are the hallmark of our ministry. A great way to draw in more people to your ministry is to provide a free resource that matches the mission of your ministry. When you look at major ministries that are non-churches, there are some major factors involved. When you go to their website, there will usually be an email list you can sign up for where you can receive free encouragement and more. What can you provide to your audience to help them go deeper into God's Word and understand the mission at hand? Ideas include scripture sheets/confessions, devotional, study guides/workbooks, online teaching with download, ect. When ministries use Facebook Ads, a very popular way to gain more visibility is to push your free opt-in for people to download and in turn they join your ministry email list. Make sure the free gift is something that many people can use and can see applying to their lives.

When it comes to how ministries can build communities locally, it goes back to what I discussed with the hair salon but on a spiritual note. You must become involved with the community and establish yourself as a resource that your target demographic can reach out to. You can host local or nationwide/global events as well that further propel the vision. Also, do not neglect the power of collaboration to reach even more people. Collaboration in ministry is another great way to connect to other people's networks. Be open (and also discerning) to collaborating with platforms that can be of help to your target audience.

A church is a ministry but the main difference is that it is planted with a pastor (covering), leadership, and members. Every church should have a distinct sound yet at the same time a oneness that links them to the body of Christ in general. What do I mean by this? There should be a unique experience people have by visiting. You don't have to re-invent the wheel but you do do need to know this question.

Question: "What do we do best and how can we use that to our advantage to win people to Christ?"

God gifts every church with amazing people who bring something to the table as members and leaders. In working with several churches, I've come to learn that many churches try to be a jack of all trades, especially in the early stages of building or re-establishing their church. Great churches focus on what they do best and they build and focus on that. As you grow, God will equip you with people who can help fill the void. Assemble your leadership team and lay out a mission for 2-3 main goals that match who you are as a church and your demographic.

APPLICATION

1. What is the mission of your ministry/church? What do you do well?

2. How can you maximize your "well" to become a staple of your ministry?

3. Based upon the past, what do you need to remove from your ministry that isn't focused on the core message nor your demographic? Are there things that you thought would reach them but truly don't?

How do we grow our church using Boss Builder strategies?

Growth in a church is seen externally and internally. Community building does both. There are so many layers to church growth and what brings people. However, let's break it down into four simple areas that create the flow.

1) The Weekend Experience & Weekday Services

When people come to your services/studies/small groups, do they leave knowing who you are and who you seek to reach? Every Sunday, make sure you communicate this in a short tagline or in your welcome to your congregation. This is also important for your members to know because they should be able to quickly give the "pitch"/invitation of who you are & who you seek to reach. If your members don't know, how can they help you reach more and more souls and families?

Flow of Service & Sermon is key to providing an experience for your guests and members. I truly believe in the supernatural and the flowing of the Holy Spirit. There are moments in a service where God takes over completely and 5 minutes becomes 30 minutes. I believe in there being the presence of the supernatural that flows with order. What do I mean by this? Most churches I know have some system of flow whether you open up with prayer or praise & worship, there is usually a flow. The Holy Spirit flows when you flow so make sure your teams are organized and equipped to serve the people walking into those church doors. Make sure teams arrive early before start of service to address any technical or sound difficulties as well as putting people in place at the guest tables, children's church, ect. When chaos is clearly seen, know that your visitors will pick it up faster than you will.

2) The Follow-Up

Once a visitor comes, what happens? Do you have a flow/ engagement system for when someone visits? There are two ways to engage with your visitors depending on the size of your church. For smaller communities, I suggest going with the good 'ole visitors card that can be filled out at the guest table before they walk into service. One of the worst things you can do is put visitors on the spot. Many times I hear from volunteers/staff is this saying. "Well how do we know who is new or a visitor if they don't stand up?" I'm shocked when people say this because your members should be hugging and embracing everyone whether member or non-member. If they feel the love and if they believe that your church is the church for them, you don't have to worry about spotting out "new faces". Everyone should be a "loving face". I also suggest that in smaller communities have 2-3 people in charge of being "spotters". These are volunteers who have the sole responsibility of greeting new faces/families just in case no one else notices.

For medium to larger sized churches, technology will be your best friend. When you have people in droves or in various sections, it's hard to spot new faces. Have a visitors table in the front of your church and use technology during announcements. A great way of using technology is to have a keyword that your visitors can text to receive a free gift such as an e-book or a link to a free audio or video just for them as a way of saying "welcome". In turn, you'll get their phone numbers and many times you can set it up so that you can also ask for their email addresses.

Once the visitor information is gathered, make sure that all visitor and membership information is stored. We'll discuss the systems and technology for that on a different day.

3) Community Development & Equipping

Growth not just seen by the amount of people coming in. It's also seen in the development of those you currently have. There is nothing more worse than having seats packed with undeveloped souls. People reach people and if you aren't reaching those you have right now, then they won't feel inspired to reach out to others. Here are some key ways to develop your members so they can see their purpose.

- Teaching on the purpose of the local body & your church specifically in the community
- Teaching on evangelism and winning others to Christ
- Teaching on spiritual development and maturing in Christ

These topics can be taught in the form of bible study, small groups, weekend services,ect. It is key that they are taught so that your community is empowered with the knowledge of their role as a member in a local body and how they are to go and bring others to church consistently.

If you develop the people, they will reach the people. You must also give them tools to reach others with. This includes postcards, creating social media graphics & quotes that they can post, and giving them prompts at the end of service or during announcements encouraging them to share with others. If you don't show them what to do, they will not do it. Example: Make it a goal that during "y" week, we're going to invite everyone to our Fall Fest so please share the flyer that we have posted on the church's social media pages. Also, in a moment, our ushers/greeters/ect. are going to pass out cards in each row for you to share with those that you know.

Bonus Tip: Asking your congregation to take flyers off the table following service rarely work. Use the tip of passing them out during service and giving it to them directly. Don't wait for them to take action. You equip them on the spot with what they need. If they don't want to take a card, they will pass it to the next person. I promise you.

4) Purposeful Activities

Not every event is worth doing. This goes back to the first day of this section where we talked about doing what you can do well. One of the ways that churches don't grow is that they do what others do. So if everyone is having a certain concert, so are you. If everyone is doing a youth explosion, so are you. The real question is: Based on who we're meant to serve and what we do best, what will help them?

It's truly about doing what your target demographic needs and not necessarily what you think is a good idea because you saw someone else do it. Help the people. When you're looking to expand your church, you need to expand the way that you think about activities.

Think about these things:
- You want the "WOW" factor but it will never be greater than the IMPACT factor. What brings people back consistently is impact. Think about children who play with toys. They may see something that is attractive and it will pull them in but what will keep them is what that item does for them on a continual basis.
- Make sure whatever you do fills a void.
- What is your impact ratio? Your impact ratio is comprised of three things: Community, Souls, Seats. How many total is your reach in your community (1 mile radius)? How many souls were won? How many people came out?

You also need to consider and think about how many people you have versus how many people are attending events. You want to make sure you have a healthy percentage so that you aren't hosting events where the attendance percentage is low. Don't just host events because you want to say that you did something. It's better to do four events every year with large impact than one every month and it has low participation and impact.

Here are some great questions to help you plan for purposeful activities for your church to reach others.

- What is the spiritual goal for this event? What is the impact goal? How will we accomplish this and in what way?
- What is the attendance goal? How will we reach the intended audience? Where are they and how can we reach them in a way that they will see our event promotion?
- How can we engage our members to help us reach the people for this event? Do we have any connections at our church to reach more than we intended?
- How can we connect to local organizations or leaders to help us push this event or garner support? Do we need to engage radio, tv, or social media ads?

APPLICATION

1. Do we need to improve our Weekend Service flow? Are our church staff/volunteers effective in their visitor engagement and follow-up?

2. Do we effectively equip our members to help us promote our events and activities?

3. Are we gauging the effectiveness of our events? How can we mix our message with the "wow" factor in order to connect with the community?

What tools do we need to manage & promote our community?

We're going to breakdown the platforms that all churches should operate with at a minimum.

1. Website
2. Giving Tool (Online & Mobile)
3. Church Membership System
4. Social Media Platforms
5. Visuals

Website

You will need to make sure you have the following: Location, Service Times, Contact Information, and Church Information. Think about having great photography, showing your members and the facility. Keep the website updated with upcoming events and celebrations including weekly services. Also, make sure the website is responsive meaning that it works well on both phone as well as computer and tablet. Be sure that the website is easy to navigate and that the headings and titles are not confusing. In the back of this workbook, you will find the resource section with links to articles, website links, and more.

Giving Tool

Churches must move towards using technology especially in giving. You want to make sure that you can use a keyword that people can text to give so that they don't need to leave the seat. Whenever you give online, know that there are transaction fees which include a percentage (usually below 5% of that total giving amount). However, that is a small price to pay for the fact that online giving increases people giving. In the back, there are a few platforms that I highly suggest looking into. Some giving tools are included in Church Membership Systems.

Church Management

This is a very important system. Every church should have a way to manage everyone who visits and is a member of your church. My favorite for small to mid-size churches is Breeze. Many also use Church Community Builder for small to mid-size as well. For mid-size to larger churches, think about Planning Center, Fellowship One, or ServantKeeper. I believe in transitioning as you grow. The worst thing to do is to pay for a very robust system that you just don't need yet. Most management systems include giving, check-ins, volunteer/staff attendance, visitor/member information, email marketing, registrations, and more.

Social Media

I suggest beginning with two platforms which are Facebook and Instagram. Anything beyond that is optional. I suggest starting with a Facebook Page and then using a Business Instagram Account if your church includes the younger generation. Use Snapchat for young adult events and YouTube to post inspirational short trailers and bumpers. Remember to use your content calendar (located in the back) to plan, schedule, and promote content. Assign a volunteer or staff member to handle all the accounts for your church. I even recommend having a staff schedule content for the pastor's pages as well so that as much that can be automated, will be.

Visuals

Every church needs a photographer and a graphic design team or individual. If you don't have an in-house one, hire one on a monthly retainer with a set budget. Paying per project can be extremely costly. Photography helps show potential visitors your church in an intimate and fresh way. I recommend taking photos monthly for at least two services per month to gather enough imagery for future promotions. Develop a library of photography that spans every year. If you can't currently hire a graphic designer, look in the back of this workbook for graphic design resources for churches. I've included various platforms that are sure to help you.

APPLICATION

1. Do a website audit and look for broken links, old information that hasn't been updated, presence of inviting photography, making sure contact links are correct, and more. Is your website responsive when you view it on the phone?

2. Do you use online/text giving? Do you use a church management system that works for you? If not, research suggested platforms in the back of the workbook and schedule a call with the company of your choice to see if they can fit your needs.

3. Are you using social media effectively? If so, how can you improve? If not, where do you need to start to make some serious changes?

I'm a Pastor. How do I engage our community consistently through my teachings?

Teaching Series are great for churches because it helps your congregation solidify the teaching in their minds and keeps them engaged on a particular subject. Again, remember the time we're living in. Repetition helps people remember. Picking a main subject that God has given you and teaching on that for an average of 4-6 weeks is a great way to keep people connected to the substance that they are getting as spiritual food. It also helps draw in visitors because for four weeks, you're sharing the same topic.

A sermon calendar is like a content calendar except it's for pastors and ministers. One of the biggest pitfalls in churches is lack of push when it comes to sermons or events. Many things are done last minute and that's not how God desires it. I suggest that leaders within the church go before God and plan at least 15-30 days in advance of what the next sermon series will be so that your leadership can be equipped to prepare the church for the next set of teachings and wise revelation from God.

Think about investing in postcards where the sermon series is on one side (just the graphic with the title and subtitle) and then on the back: a description of what the series is about, location w/ map & service times. I don't suggest doing this every time you have a new series. Usually 3-4 times a year is good so that it's not bringing in unnecessary expenses.

I've included a copy of a basic sermon calendar on the following page to walk you through how to easily organize your sermons for maximum impact and in turn help your church marketing team be prepared to share on social media, in email, and using print materials.

Sermon Calendar for Month:_____ Year:_____

Name of the Series:

Subtitle: Optional but can be a huge benefit

The Big Idea (for the Series): *This a 2-3 description of the sermon series that you can use to promote leading up to the next series and for marketing.*

Scriptures:

Notes:

Example Sermon Calendar

Sermon Calendar for Month:_____ Year:_____
Example Series: Look Into the Stars
Subtitle: Discover How to Walk By Faith In the Midst of Darkness
Example Big Idea: *God keeps His promises; we must remain obedient to Him even when the future isn't clear. Join us as we dive into a series about a man called Abraham who had to learn how to look into the stars and discover faith!*
    Scriptures:
    Notes:

Week 1 : Series: Look to the Stars

Text: Genesis 12:1-9
Topic: Obedience, Blessing
Big Idea: Your obedience to God can be used to bless others, some of whom you may never meet.
    Scriptures:
    Notes:

Week 2 : Series: Look to the Stars

Text: Genesis 15
Topic: God's Promises, Redemption
Big Idea: God's promises can be trusted.
    Scriptures:
    Notes:

Week 3: Series: Look to the Stars

Text: Genesis 18:22-33

Topic: Justice, Mercy

Big Idea: Because God is holy and just, He takes sin seriously. Yet, we find that He is also full of grace and mercy, giving humanity many opportunities to repent.

Scriptures:

Notes:

Week 4: Series: Look to the Stars

Text: Genesis 22

Topic: Sacrifice, Obedience, God's Promises

Big Idea: Abraham trusted the faithfulness of God even when it was difficult.

Scriptures:

Notes:

APPLICATION

1. Pastors: Do you currently teach through monthly sermon themes (sermon series)? If not, how can you create a flow for your church including your creative team? Remember, if your creative team is alerted in advance of upcoming series, it will make their job easier.

2. What is your next upcoming series? What are the main themes? Will you contact your creative team so that they can produce graphics, online material, and more to help push the series?

How do we use social media to expand our reach?

Social media isn't meant to be used as a bulletin board. Yes, it's the place where we announce upcoming events and weekly services but there's so much more potential. Social media provides a gateway for your ministry to attract a greater audience.

1. Turn Your Church Into A Resource

The internet can be a great way to draw in visitors who will soon become members. Think about YouTube to place sermons with good titles. Think about Facebook for the main headquarters of online content and Instagram for more visual content such as photography based content. Make your ministry page become a place where people come daily for inspiration.

2. Create Engaging Content Based on Current Sermon Series

When creating content, infuse the current sermon series to bring the message alive. Think about the main key points from the previous week and build out inspiration surrounding the theme. What scriptures stood out? What quotes would be perfect for a graphic post? Think about turning one of the sermons into a quick blog post such as "5 Ways to Jumpstart Your Prayer Life" if there is a current teaching on prayer. You can also think about "10 Scriptures For A

Successful Fast" when you're doing a series on fasting. You can post these on your website and then share them on social media as a resource to your followers. Tell your members to become engaged with your social media accounts.

3. Create A Free Resource for email subscribers

A great idea for a church or ministry is to think about your vision and mission for your church and create a resource from it. Think about doing a free download of a sermon message, confession/ scripture sheet download, encouragement e-book,ect. It should give them a preview of what they will experience. You can run FB Ads that target this Free Resource to people near your church. This is a great way to connect to local potential visitors and reach them with a gift.

APPLICATION

1. How can you prevent your ministry from becoming a bulletin board and more of an engager of content?

2. What kind of resource can your ministry offer as a free downloadable gift for them when they come onto your social media or website? *Be sure that they provide their email in exchange for the free gift :)*

3. What kind of resources will you provide on a monthly basis? (Example: 1 blog post per month, daily social media content, videos,ect.)

FACEBOOK BASICS

FOR CHURCHES & MINISTRIES

GENESIS DORSEY

TABLE OF CONTENTS

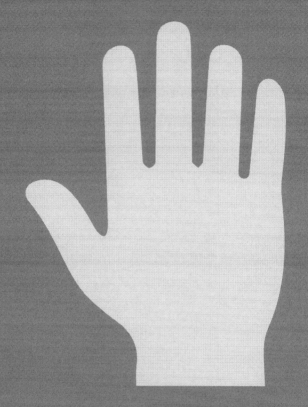

THE INTRODUCTION

BECAUSE IT'S RUDE NOT FOR ME TO SAY HELLO TO YOU!

HELLO!

Who am I? I'm a Pastor's Kid based out of Delaware that has a passion for helping churches and small businesses connect with people and turning those people ultimately to Jesus Christ.

I've spent countless hours working with churches and their staff on social media. The fun part is set of steps. People love to start things. However, when you have to put in daily work to keep it consistently going, the fun seems to fade away.

Well guess what? It doesn't have to be like that. If you're someone who genuinely believes that social media can help your church (which it can), then this e-book is just for you! In this book, I break down tips on establish a well-designed page and create awesome content to keep your members and potential visitors coming back. Are you ready to learn? Let's go!

1

WHY FACEBOOK?

IT'S KIND OF A BIG DEAL

WHY?

ACCORDING TO PEW RESEARCH, HERE ARE THE STATS...

- 71% of all online adults use Facebook.
- 58% of the entire adult population use Facebook
- 66% of all online men use Facebook
- 77% of all online women use Facebook
- 87% of all online 18-29 year olds use Facebook
- 73% of all online 30-49 year olds use Facebook
- 63% of all online 50-64 year olds use Facebook
- 56% of all online 65+ year olds use Facebook

The point is that everyone is on Facebook. I believe that every church should have a Facebook page. In addition, it's a great "first" for a social media account for your church. It offers the ability to post pictures, statuses, videos of different length, and live streaming.

It's a great way to get the news out about upcoming events, classes, online giving, past and upcoming sermons, and more. Have I convinced you enough? Well, let's talk about setting your page up!

2

THE SETUP

LEARN WHAT NEEDS TO BE ON YOUR
PAGE AND WHAT YOU NEED TO REMOVE

THE PAGE

LET'S GO OVER WHAT YOU NEED...

The first thing you need to do is make sure it's setup as a PAGE and not a PERSONAL PROFILE. The worst thing I hate to see is when a church sends me a "friend request". Nothing should be hidden when it comes to an organization. Someone with a personal Facebook Profile must create the page. Facebook doesn't allow businesses to create their own pages anymore. The easiest way to get around this is to create a personal Facebook account for your creative team. A fun thing to do is come up with a "invisble team member" for your creative team and create a Facebook Personal Account for your invisible mascot. Then setup a Facebook Page through this account. When starting up with a small or non-existent Creative Team this is the best route.

How do I create a Page?

Desktop Help   Mobile Browser Help   Other Help Centers ▾   ➔ Share Article

Pages are for businesses, brands and organizations to share their stories and connect with people. Like profiles, you can customize a Page by publishing stories, hosting events and more. People who like your Page and their friends can get updates in News Feed.

To create a Page:

1   Go to facebook.com/pages/create

2   Click to choose a Page category

3   Select a more specific category from the dropdown menu and fill out the required information

4   Click **Get Started** and follow the on-screen instructions

Now let's go over what you need to include on this page. You're doing a great job so far!

THE PAGE

LET'S GO OVER WHAT YOU NEED...

Depending on your Page's category, you can add different types of basic info. For example, if your Page's category is **Local Businesses**, you can add your address, phone number and more info about your business.

To add info to your Page:

1 Click **About** on the left side of your Page

2 Click **Page Info**

3 Click the section you want to edit and add info

4 Click **Save Changes**

This info will appear in your Page's **About** section and on the right side of your Page's Timeline.

Make sure you include all necessary in the "About" section. Make sure that you are marked as a Religious Organization if you are a church or ministry.

If you are making a page as a pastor or preacher, note it as Public Figure.

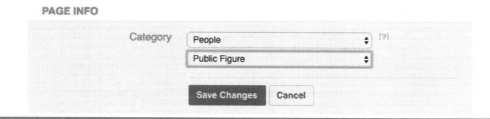

THE PAGE

LET'S GO OVER WHAT YOU NEED...

Depending on your Page's category, you can add different types of basic info. For example, if your Page's category is **Local Businesses**, you can add your address, phone number and more info about your business.

To add info to your Page:

1   Click **About** on the left side of your Page

2   Click **Page Info**

3   Click the section you want to edit and add info

4   Click **Save Changes**

This info will appear in your Page's **About** section and on the right side of your Page's Timeline.

Make sure you include all necessary in the "About" section. Make sure that you are marked as a Religious Organization if you are a church or ministry.

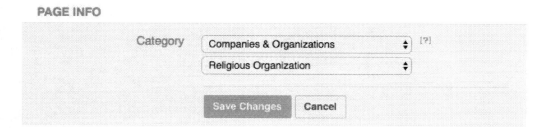

If you are making a page as a pastor or preacher, note it as Public Figure.

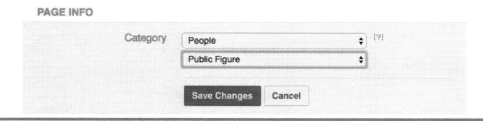

3

DESIGN RULES

TIME TO THROW THAT CREATIVE
ANOINTING ON YOUR PAGE

DESIGN

IS WHAT SEPARATES THE AMAZING FROM THE NOT SO GOOD

Now that you have your information imported, it's time for you to upload your two main basics and we'll go from there.

1. Facebook Profile Picture & Banner

Facebook Banner: 851 pixels x 315 pixels
Facebook Profile Picture: At least 180 pixels x 180 pixels (Make sure it's sized as a square)

I've included a few designs that I've done to give you an idea of what to place as your Facebook Banner. You can promote an upcoming event, your overall year's theme, sermon series,ect.

Freedom

LEARN HOW TO LIVE A GRACE-FILLED LIFE!
MAY 28TH @ 12 NOON

NEW YEAR. NEW TIMES.

SUNDAY @ 9AM
WEDNESDAY @ 6PM

welcome

Royal Girl
WEEKEND
WASHINGTON, DC

SEPTEMBER 9-10, 2016

Registration includes Hotel, Food, and Fun!

Deadline: August 31, 2016 @ 11:59 PM EST

GIRLSOFROYALTY.COM/TRIPS

4

THE 80/20 RULE

YOUR CHURCH IS NOT AN
ADVERTISEMENT CENTER. BE HUMAN.

80/20

80% INSPIRATION. 20% PROMOTION.

The problem for many churches when working with their social media strategies is that they forget about being human. People don't follow pages for just updates. They want to be inspired. Content that is inspirational has a higher percentage of getting shared than a flyer.

However, becoming a platform that shares hope will increase your 20% of promotion being shared much more.

80% Inspiration
+ Daily Bible verse
+ Inspirational quotes
+ Sermon quotes, responses or previews
+ Volunteer/member feature
+ Throwback Thursday photo
+ Photo albums of church events
+ Thanks & shout-outs to volunteers & staff
+ Church-related hashtags

20% Promotion
+ Flyers, Upcoming Events, Announcements

80/20

80% INSPIRATION. 20% PROMOTION.

TYPES OF CONTENT
+ Photo based
+ Video based
+ Text Based

Daily Inspiration Ideas
+ Graphic showcasing scripture

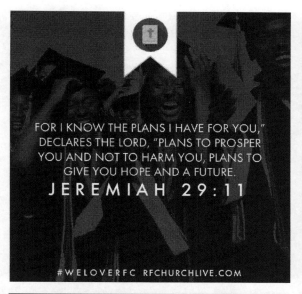

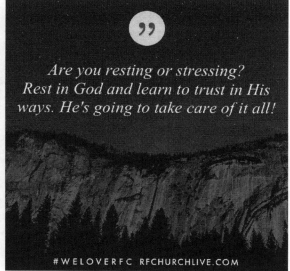

80/20

80% INSPIRATION. 20% PROMOTION.

I think it's a good balance (especially when starting out), to go from text based inspiration and then include graphics (like these below) to sprinkle in between. You can find images like this on Google.

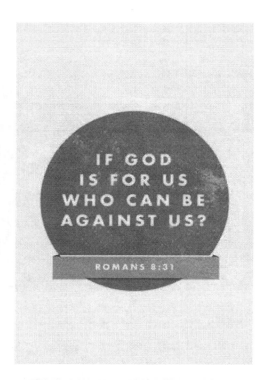

80/20

80% INSPIRATION. 20% PROMOTION.

For sermon quotes, my local church uses WordSwag to create quick on-the-go Graphics. We also use the Over App as well. We're able to create sermon graphics in under 2 minutes flat.

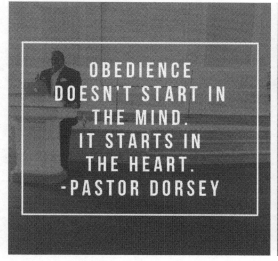

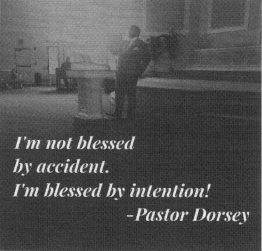

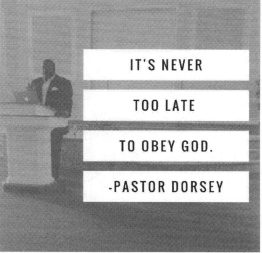

5

ENGAGEMENT

IT'S TIME TO GET THE PEOPLE SHARING,
LIKING, AND SPREADING THE WORD!

ENGAGE

IT'S TIME TO GET THE PEOPLE INTERACTING WITH YOUR PAGE

Make sure to infuse your social media into regular promotions at your church or ministry including physical and online. Encourage people to follow you on social media including visitors. Invite your members to share the page to their Facebook Friends.

If you're creating awesome content like we touched on in the past chapter, people will begin to share your content. That content will show up in other's people's feeds that you did not have access to. This is called building awareness for your church. It is not an overnight process and takes time. However, I know that you will do an amazing job growing the page and attracting people to your ministry!

Creating inspiring content is really key. Remember to be consistent, try to post at least once a day every week. You can do it!

ENGAGE

IT'S TIME TO GET THE PEOPLE INTERACTING WITH YOUR PAGE

You can also increase engagement by doing Facebook Ads or Boosting specific posts that are getting great attention. We suggest you promote upcoming events or a quote from a sermon. You can also boost a video. For videos, the suggestion is to boost a story about why someone fell in love with your church or a clip from a recent sermon that is short & to the point. For Facebook Ads, you can set your own budget for as low as $5! So definitely experiment with doing 1-2 Facebook Ads per month for either a quote or a video.

People love to see themselves! Get someone to volunteer as the church photographer and post pictures from service on the Facebook Page in an album labeled with the date. People want to see who attends your church. Putting human faces to the ministry is an awesome way to show the human side of your social media page.

ENGAGE

IT'S TIME TO GET THE PEOPLE
INTERACTING WITH YOUR PAGE

Not everything belongs on a Facebook
Page. What will decrease engagement is
when you post announcements that may
not need to be for public display.

When it comes to posting "Events", be sure
to NOT post weekly services as separate
upcoming events. That's not necessary.
Only use it to promote major upcoming
events and be sure to not promote last
minute. Encourage people to share and
promote your upcoming events with you!

Create special hype around certain days.
This is not for every church. However, this
may work for yours. I worked with one
church that created "Monday's Inspiration"
where their pastor shared a 1 minute video
JUST for Facebook. The church posted it to
the FB page every Monday and it grew into
something special.

6

FACEBOOK LIVE

LEARN HOW TO UTILIZE FACEBOOK LIVE

GO LIVE

USE FACEBOOK LIVE TO ENGAGE

Going Live with Facebook

1. Tap "What's on your mind" at the top of News Feed.

2. Select "Live Video" from the dropdown menu.

 **Live Video**

3. Add a description and choose your audience before hitting "Go Live." You'll see a three-second countdown before your broadcast begins!

Facebook Live is an awesome tool to help you connect with your audience in REAL TIME. However, you don't want to use this without having a plan in place.

1. Use a phone that has great camera quality + use a tri-pod to put it on
2. Tell people ahead of time when you're going live
3. Write in the description box what they are watching during this live broadcast
4. Ask your LIVE viewers to follow you and share the live feed (Do NOT do this if you're sharing a live sermon or teaching. ONLY do this if this is a behind-the-scenes or sit-down talk directly with the FB audience)

GO LIVE

USE FACEBOOK LIVE TO ENGAGE

+ Facebook Live videos can last up to 90 Minutes (so if you're doing a live stream for your church, keep this in mind)

You can connect the API from Facebook to create professionally streamed content.

See this link to see FB Live Partners: https://www.facebook.com/facebookmedia/get-started/live-video-solutions

Talk to your video tech team at your church on how you can make this happen.

Use iPads to capture small church sessions and up close capture to go Live.

https://switcherstudio.com/en/learn-more/go-live

Consult your church tech team to figure out which method would be best for Facebook Live. Take full advantage of this feature!

7

TIME TO SCHEDULE

LEARN HOW TO NOT WASTE TIME SCHEDULING CONTENT

SCHEDULE

LEARN HOW TO SAVE TIME WITH AUTOMATION & SCHEDULING CONTENT

When I first posted content, I thought that I had to open my phone every time. However, as your church grows (or maybe it's already large and growing), you need time to work on other things. This is where using a scheduler platform comes in handy.

Platform: Buffer or HootSuite
Buffer is (in my opinion) the #1 online platform (also available as an app) for churches to use for content scheduling for Facebook. In my opinion, it doesn't get any simpler than this. It allows you to schedule the time and days for your content. It also posts on your behalf. So you don't have to be present to post. Isn't that awesome? Another great thing that these platforms provide is statistics to let you know what times work best to post. You want to figure out the best strategy for your audience. These platforms will tell you when your audience is most receptive to see and engage with your content.

SCHEDULE

LEARN HOW TO SAVE TIME WITH AUTOMATION & SCHEDULING CONTENT

Calendar: Handwritten then Digital

As you grow, you want to make it a practice to create a content calendar for your content. I create my calendar as a monthly calendar and layout content Sunday-Saturday with the time, type of content, and what I'm actually posting. What seems to work for many churches is to section off each day and keep it consistent.

Larger churches that I have worked with to setup their posting schedules include posting 4-5 times a day. Being that my own church is small church, I'm not going to use my larger church strategy for my volunteer position at my small church. We post a few times a week being that I attend a church that is just falling into the social media wave. Don't rush your people but be sure to post content every week. I write down my ideas for the week and then turn it into an online calendar so that someone can easily come in and see my plan for the week.

8

FINAL THOUGHTS

1. FACEBOOK IS WHERE YOU NEED TO BE
2. SHARE HOPE WITH 20% PROMOTION
3. BE CONSISTENT IN POSTING & ENGAGE
4. TAKE ADVANTAGE OF FACEBOOK LIVE
5. SCHEDULE YOUR CONTENT & SAVE TIME

MOST IMPORTANTLY,
DO IT ALL UNTO GOD & KNOW THAT YOUR
HARD WORK HELPS IN WINNING SOULS!

THANKS FOR READING!

HEY IT'S GENESIS AGAIN AND I'M SO HAPPY THAT YOU'VE MADE TIME TO READ THIS RESOURCE. IF YOU HAVE ANY QUESTIONS, FEEL FREE TO REACH OUT AND EMAIL ME AT INFO@GENESISDORSEY.COM.

VISIT MY WEBSITE:
GENESISDORSEY.COM

WANT TO BOOK ME FOR A CONFERENCE OR SEMINAR? EMAIL MY TEAM TODAY!
BOOKING@GENESISDORSEY.COM

How does a church use a content calendar in planning for effective communication?

Content calendar planning is key. This is a role that your church's or ministry's creative team or director is in charge of organizing and executing. Let's break down how to create a content calendar for a church. It's similar to how it's done for business owners but a bit different.

1. What's the focus for this month? (Sermon Series)
2. What events are happening this month? (Dates)
3. What are our platforms of reach? (Website (Blog), Email Marketing, Social Media, Church Services/Events)
    1. How many times will we post on each social media platform? What kinds of content will we post?
    2. How many emails will we send our congregation & visitors per week? (One per week is great)

A church's content calendar is much simpler than a business because the content is being taken from a consistent message. It's a blessing because sermons are filled with tons of content. Pulling 30 second to 1 minute video and audio clips are perfect to share on social media as videos.

See content calendar in the back for resource.

Serve on the creative team for your church? Here are your goals for every week.

1. What great quotes came from this week's sermon?
2. What needs to go in this week's email?
3. How far are we on next month's theme & focus?
4. What has the pastor sent us that we need to be working on now? Do we need to update anything on the website or other platforms this week?
5. Make sure to respond to any online comments

APPLICATION

1. Do you currently have a church content calendar? If yes, how can you improve the calendar? If no, what do your first steps need to be?

2. What social media platforms are you currently on? Are you integrating weekly encouragement? Are you directing your audience to those platforms?

3. How can you increase your ministry's involvement with social media? (Example: Prompting them to post pictures, hashtags, check-in on Facebook,ect.)

COMMUNICATE
AN EASY GUIDE FOR BASIC COMMUNICATIONS FOR CHURCHES & BUSINESSES

WEB

What system do you currently use for your website? Is it easy to maintain? When was the last time you updated your system? Is it a responsive site? (A site that adapts to whatever screen it is being shown on- mobile, tablet,desktop,ect.)

LOGO

What does your current logo look like? Is it simple? Can it be used over and over again? Is it unique and not like any other ministry? Is it being used on your website, flyers, and more? Is it being consistently used so that people can easily describe what it looks like from memory?

NEW CONTENT

Do you refresh the content that is on your website? Do you blog and update your events or calendar? Do people struggle trying to find information easily? Have you asked several people to do a test where you ask them to locate specific information on your site and time them to see how long it takes them? Can people easily find your contact information including physical location, if applicable?

COPYRIGHT

Do you have a copyright on your website or any important information? Is it updated to the current year?

TAGLINE

What is the tagline or phrase for your brand? Is it easy to memorize? Do you share it and show it frequently?

EMAIL/MAIL

How do you communicate with others? Is it email, social media, direct mailers, regular mailing, or text messaging? Do you have a calendar or plan per month on what type of content and how often you will share it?

TIMING & AMOUNT

Do you overwhelm people with upcoming events or content? Are you begging people to engage or is it more of an invitation? Are you providing value? Are you truly listening to your audience? Is what you are providing relevant to your demographic?

LAST MINUTE TIPS

Here is the truth. Whether or not you wish to communicate, you are communicating something good or bad. Absence speaks. Show up and be present. It will take work. What you do not know, find someone who does and eventually build a team.

What should a church website include? What kind of platform should we use?

A church website should include these following basics:

1. Service Times
2. Location (map) & Contact Information
3. About the Church & Statement of Believes (What You Believe)
4. About Leadership (Greeting from Pastor(s))
5. History/Story of Church (The Why)
6. Upcoming Events & How people can engage with you
7. Links/Icons to social media pages
8. Photography showing church community (quality shots)

The homepage is the most important page of your website because it's the welcoming page to visitors. Make sure that the home page has a welcoming message that gives a very short summary of what your church is about. You'll see examples shortly to see how different church execute on their home page.

Here are some things to consider adding to your church website to showcase who you're destined to help.

1. Testimonies to showcase what God has done in their life or Member stories to highlight how attending the church has changed their life.

2.   Make sure your website expresses how you are here to help the people. Don't brag about how awesome you are. Brag about how excited you are to help those who attend your church.

When building your church website, it all depends on your budget. The most popular platforms include Squarespace and Wordpress for easy to setup websites. If you don't have it in your budget for website maintenance or a large website budget in the thousands, I highly suggest Squarespace.

Here are some example sites using Squarespace:
1.   http://www.greenhousesouthflorida.org/
2.   https://rockvillechurchofchrist.org/
3.   http://www.theactionchurch.com/
4.   http://www.firstchurch.com/
5.   http://www.rfchurchlive.com/
6.   http://churchatredriver.com/
7.   http://www.citychurchchicago.com/

Here are some examples using Wordpress:
1.   http://gracehillschurch.com/
2.   https://epic.church/
3.   http://lhc.org/
4.   http://calvarychatt.com/
5.   https://enjoy.church/
6.   http://www.questchurchstl.org/
7.   http://gladtidingsomaha.com/

APPLICATION

1. Do a website audit for your church if you have a website. According to the list of things that every church should have, do you have those things?

2. Does your church website scream "We're here for you" or "We're here for us"? What sections can you re-write to appeal more to the visitor?

3. Do you have a collection of church photography to use for social media, the website, flyers, and more? If not, hire a photographer to come in for your next four services or to come in once every 3 months for an entire year to build up a large library of photos. It's well worth the investment.

How can personally branding leadership help the church?

Personally branding your church leadership is a great way to expand the reach of your church. However, this should only be done at the correct pace. If your leadership is open, think about leadership being present on social media to connect to the world.

Having leadership do online social media live streams concerning prayer, encouragement, and dialogue is a great way for the world to meet your leadership virtually. It gives them an off-the-pulpit view of your leaders and establishes trust. If your leaders don't want to do too much social media, I suggest scheduling their content including scheduling some church announcements to also be posted to their account. Pastoral/Minister accounts can be monitored by a church member. However, whoever manages ministry accounts must have a certain level of discretion and must be extremely trustworthy.

Here are some fun things your leadership can do during the week to engage with more people via social media.

1. Weekly Encouragement
2. Live Streaming Short Bible Study
3. Behind-the-scenes with Pastor/Minister (insert name)
4. Q&A Live Chats
5. Sermon Recap Video

APPLICATION

1. Do you brand your leadership outside engaging outside of weekend services?

2. How can you bring your leadership to connect with the everyday life of your members & visitors using online engagement?

3. Talk to your leadership about introducing short engagement periods with the leadership and the social media community.

SECTION FOUR

RESOURCE SECTION

Entire Year Content Calendar & Notes

You can either break down your content into 12 Months (12 Focuses) or into Quarters (4 Focuses with a sub-focus per month) or into any other customized way. Try to keep it simple.

CONTENT IDEA SECTION

Use this area to write out ideas for content ideas and topics

Month

20 ◯

Sunday	Monday	Tuesday	Wednesday	Thursday	Friday	Saturday
◯	◯	◯	◯	◯	◯	◯
◯	◯	◯	◯	◯	◯	◯
◯	◯	◯	◯	◯	◯	◯
◯	◯	◯	◯	◯	◯	◯
◯	◯	◯	◯	◯	◯	◯
◯	◯	◯	◯	◯	◯	◯

Month

20

Sunday	Monday	Tuesday	Wednesday	Thursday	Friday	Saturday

Month [   ] 20 ◯

Sunday	Monday	Tuesday	Wednesday	Thursday	Friday	Saturday
◯	◯	◯	◯	◯	◯	◯
◯	◯	◯	◯	◯	◯	◯
◯	◯	◯	◯	◯	◯	◯
◯	◯	◯	◯	◯	◯	◯
◯	◯	◯	◯	◯	◯	◯
◯	◯	◯	◯	◯	◯	◯

Month

20

Sunday	Monday	Tuesday	Wednesday	Thursday	Friday	Saturday

Month

20

Sunday	Monday	Tuesday	Wednesday	Thursday	Friday	Saturday
◯	◯	◯	◯	◯	◯	◯
◯	◯	◯	◯	◯	◯	◯
◯	◯	◯	◯	◯	◯	◯
◯	◯	◯	◯	◯	◯	◯
◯	◯	◯	◯	◯	◯	◯
◯	◯	◯	◯	◯	◯	◯

Month

20 ◯

Sunday	Monday	Tuesday	Wednesday	Thursday	Friday	Saturday
◯	◯	◯	◯	◯	◯	◯
◯	◯	◯	◯	◯	◯	◯
◯	◯	◯	◯	◯	◯	◯
◯	◯	◯	◯	◯	◯	◯
◯	◯	◯	◯	◯	◯	◯
◯	◯	◯	◯	◯	◯	◯

Month

20

Sunday	Monday	Tuesday	Wednesday	Thursday	Friday	Saturday
○	○	○	○	○	○	○
○	○	○	○	○	○	○
○	○	○	○	○	○	○
○	○	○	○	○	○	○
○	○	○	○	○	○	○
○	○	○	○	○	○	○

Month

20 ◯

Sunday	Monday	Tuesday	Wednesday	Thursday	Friday	Saturday
◯	◯	◯	◯	◯	◯	◯
◯	◯	◯	◯	◯	◯	◯
◯	◯	◯	◯	◯	◯	◯
◯	◯	◯	◯	◯	◯	◯
◯	◯	◯	◯	◯	◯	◯
◯	◯	◯	◯	◯	◯	◯

Month

20

Sunday	Monday	Tuesday	Wednesday	Thursday	Friday	Saturday
○	○	○	○	○	○	○
○	○	○	○	○	○	○
○	○	○	○	○	○	○
○	○	○	○	○	○	○
○	○	○	○	○	○	○
○	○	○	○	○	○	○

Month [ ] 20 ( )

Sunday	Monday	Tuesday	Wednesday	Thursday	Friday	Saturday
( )	( )	( )	( )	( )	( )	( )
( )	( )	( )	( )	( )	( )	( )
( )	( )	( )	( )	( )	( )	( )
( )	( )	( )	( )	( )	( )	( )
( )	( )	( )	( )	( )	( )	( )
( )	( )	( )	( )	( )	( )	( )

Month

20

Sunday	Monday	Tuesday	Wednesday	Thursday	Friday	Saturday
○	○	○	○	○	○	○
○	○	○	○	○	○	○
○	○	○	○	○	○	○
○	○	○	○	○	○	○
○	○	○	○	○	○	○
○	○	○	○	○	○	○

Month

20 ◯

Sunday	Monday	Tuesday	Wednesday	Thursday	Friday	Saturday
◯	◯	◯	◯	◯	◯	◯
◯	◯	◯	◯	◯	◯	◯
◯	◯	◯	◯	◯	◯	◯
◯	◯	◯	◯	◯	◯	◯
◯	◯	◯	◯	◯	◯	◯
◯	◯	◯	◯	◯	◯	◯

YEAR OF TOPICS

January _____ | Topic:

February _____ | Topic:

March _____ | Topic:

April _____ | Topic:

May _____ | Topic:

June _____ | Topic:

July _____ | Topic:

August _____ | Topic:

September _____ | Topic:

October _____ | Topic:

November _____ | Topic:

December _____ | Topic:

MONTHLY TOPICS

This Month's Topic:

Year:

Break down Weekly Topics:

Week 1:

Week 2:

Week 3:

Week 4:

(Optional) Week 5:

Blog Content Topics? (Include Posting Dates)

Video/Social Media Live Stream Topics? (Include Dates)

Email Marketing Campaigns For This Month

Remember One email per week at a minimum

Email #_____

Subject of Email:

What are the basic key points you want to cover in the email?

What's the goal for this email?

Date to Schedule It:

Email #_____

Subject of Email:

What are the basic key points you want to cover in the email?

What's the goal for this email?

Date to Schedule It:

Email #_____

Subject of Email:

What are the basic key points you want to cover in the email?

What's the goal for this email?

Date to Schedule It:

Email #_____

Subject of Email:

What are the basic key points you want to cover in the email?

What's the goal for this email?

Date to Schedule It:

Email #_____

Subject of Email:

What are the basic key points you want to cover in the email?

What's the goal for this email?

Date to Schedule It:

Email #_____

Subject of Email:

What are the basic key points you want to cover in the email?

What's the goal for this email?

Date to Schedule It:

Example Social Media Content Calendar & Notes

Auto-Scheduling Platforms
Instagram: Grum.co
Facebook Page & Group: Buffer.com

Scheduling Platforms (with reminders)
- (All Platforms) Buffer.com
- (Instagram) Later.com
- (Instagram) Planoloy.com
- (All Platforms) Crowdfire.com

September
2 Times A Day = 7 Quotes & 7 Graphics/Photos/Videos
12 Noon EST & 6 PM EST

September's Focus: Speaker Graphics + Lifestyle Posts + Quotes
- Faith & Purpose
- Relationships & Family
- Ministry
- Career & Business
- Finance
- Health & Wellness

7 Quotes (To be posted on social media)
- "If you don't like something, change it. If you can't change it, change your attitude." – Maya Angelou
- "Living in the moment means letting go of the past and not waiting for the future. It means living your life consciously, aware that each moment you breathe is a gift." – Oprah Winfrey
- "Whatever is bringing you down, get rid of it. Because you'll find that when you're free . . . your true self comes out." — Tina Turner
- "Winning is great, sure, but if you are really going to do something in life, the secret is learning how to lose. Nobody goes undefeated all the time. If you can pick up after a crushing defeat, and go on to win again, you are going to be a champion someday." – Wilma Rudolph
- "You're not obligated to win. You're obligated to keep trying to do the best you can every day." – Marian Wright Edelman
- "You are on the eve of a complete victory. You can't go wrong. The world is behind you." – Josephine Baker

Revival Fellowship Church Holiday Plan (Example)

Fonts: Futura, Sverige Script

Goals
- Excite members with festive appearance for the holiday season
- Create intrigue for visitors w/branded messages & social media engagement w/Pastors
- Create memorable experiences with families with holiday activities

Branding
- Idea: The feeling of festive energy with authority and power (colors that note this)
- Colors: Purple, Blue, and Gold & Fonts: Futura and Sverige

Implementation: 31 Days of Praise
- Daily Social Media Posts with different scriptures with pictures from the pastors
- Every Monday (Dec.5,12,19 & 25): Monday Morning w/ Pastor & First Lady Dorsey
    - Pre-recorded 3-5 minute encouraging videos (sharable content)
    - Pushing them to visit website download the 31 Day Devotional

Calendar Breakdown: 31 Days of Praise
- December 4th, 11th, 18th (Sundays to promote upcoming Holiday Events)
    • Download the 31 Day Devotional
- December 25th (Casual Sunday & Christmas Sunday)
    • Free Family Photos After Service
- December 31st-Jan.1st (New Years' Weekend-Saturday & Sunday)
    • Saturday: New Years' Eve Service
        - Special Praise & Worship Experience
        - Ice Cream Bar
    • Sunday: New Years' Day
        - Sunday Service
        - Fellowship Dinner after service ($5 Entry-MUST RSVP)

Example Email Campaigns
Copy for Boss Builder Landing Page (On Website)

GROW YOUR PLATFORM & GROW IN GOD

BECOME A BOSS BUILDER

OVER 1,000 PEOPLE HAVE SIGNED UP.
GET MY FREE 2-DAY TRAINING SENT STRAIGHT TO YOUR INBOX

When it comes to creating a stream of income through your business, your community is the key. We all need a tribe. Learn how to build your tribe in 30 days and maximize your profit. We're going to cover sharpening your opt-ins, upgrading your sales mentality for conversion, and more!

Create your community and position yourself to live the life and create the income you've always dreamed of.

(insert email inbox for sign-up)

Email for Email Subscribers to Join Boss Builder
Subject: Join Me For Two FREE Days Of Tribe Building Training!

it's time to run...
I'm excited about where you're going. God is taking you higher and higher like never before. I know that I don't know everything (what a relief) but what I do know, I know it's my duty to teach you.

I know how to create communities. It's what I do for myself and for clients. You are a part of my community. That's how you're able to read this email right now. I want to teach you how to build a community in the next 30 days.

Guess how much my training will cost you? Nothing. That's right. It's FREE.

You're going to learn the following...

- How to Create & Strategically Implement Opt-Ins
- How I easily design my offerings to grow my email list

- How to setup FB & IG ads to grow your email list
- How to convert people who came for free into customers
- How to create a consistent flow to keep your tribe members coming back
- How to grow your influence via email marketing & collaborations

Join me August 30-31 for this two day training at 9 PM EST and transform the way you build your tribe!

Click here to register

Free Opt-In Welcome Email

The time has come! Are you excited?

Login to your private learning area so you can become an official Boss Builder!

Access Link: (insert link)
Password: (insert password)

Day 1 Training is devoted to those that are....
- Confused on how to build a tribe
- Struggling on how to sell yourself and your story
- Need to gain clarity on creating the offer, the funnel, and the conversion
- How to create an opt-in & FB Ads to create leads

Day 2 Training is devoted to those that are....
- Already setup with funnels, a website, and more but things are not clicking
- Having a hard time charging your worth
- Trying to figure out ways to diversify your offerings, services, and products
- Creatives who own a one-man digital agency and can't generate enough profit to scale

I'm also going to send you even more tips in the next few weeks to help you grow your community. We're in this for the long-term my friend!

As a bonus, I've included some note taking sheets while you watch the training.

Click here to download note-taking sheets

Sincerely,
Genesis Dorsey

Welcome Email to Tribe

Hey there (insert name),

Thanks for signing up for the Boss Builder free community! I'm very passionate about helping people grow their businesses and ministries. Creating a database of your users, supporters, etc. is very important.

People ignore building up their future client or audience list. Here is a perfect example. It's 2 a.m. and you're fast asleep. Sally is surfing the web and because she's in California it's only 11 p.m. for her. She finds your Instagram or Twitter profile and is loving your social media pages. She clicks the link in your bio (because of course your website link is there-duh!). She's loving your products/services/etc. but maybe she's not an instant buyer.

But OH NO! There isn't a "stay connected" or "subscribe today" opt-in for her to type in her email address. If Sally really loves your brand, she might bookmark your site. However, most people don't. You wake up in the morning as the roosters sing their song (or maybe that's just your weird alarm app you downloaded).You have a new product that's coming out and your only plan is social media. What about Sally? How can you get in contact with Sally? What if Sally isn't on Instagram or with her "twitter peeps" and misses your announcement that you put out to social media?

Maybe it isn't the product. Maybe it's a book, course, event, or whatever else you push out. You can't continue to pour out your amazing information into an empty room. It's time to build up your platform using what you already have.

What about after they join your community? How do you keep them coming back? How do you keep them in love with what you're providing? I want to help you with that. More importantly, I want to help you grow and scale for success.

If you haven't already, log in to your special Boss Builder Training Area so you can dive into your Free 2-Day Course that I sent you. Need to access it again?

Login: (insert link)
Password: (insert password)

Talk to you soon!

Sincerely,
Genesis Dorsey

Blog Post Announcement Email
Title: Marketing Tips for Non-Fiction Christian Authors

It's Thursday! A few weeks ago, I did a Q&A session on my Instagram Live and one of the questions was about how to market your book if you're a Christian Author. I loved that question so much because many people talk about promoting but there isn't any information or ideas to execute. I had a scheduled blog post that was supposed to go out yesterday but I pulled the plug and got all of my ideas together to give Christian Authors an article that you can read and hopefully apply to your upcoming book releases.

It includes links, tips, and more. Let me know if it helps you in any way. I'm always looking for feedback AND new ideas. So if you want any insight on a topic, just let me know by responding back to this email.

Click here to read today's article on how you can apply strategy to your new book release!

Repurpose Content/Sharing Social Media Video
Title:How To Praise Out Your Prison!

What happens when you're put into an unfair circumstance...

You can only wonder how Paul and Silas were feeling in Acts 16:16-40. Talk about purpose in the midst of your prison.

There are three P's: Purpose, Prison, and Praise.

I did an Instagram Live (@gigihepburn) at midnight and I want you to have access to the teaching. I was in my funny mode and I mentioned something about macaroni & cheese and relationships. We had fun. Haha.

Click here to listen to the audio

Click here to download the worksheets

P.S. If you missed my vision video all about the upcoming Led to Lead Conference, click here to watch. If you haven't followed us on Instagram, be sure to do so at @ledtoleadconference.

Love,
Genesis Dorsey

T-Shirt Class Sales Announcement
Title: Turn $100 into $1K this month!

Hustle Work Ethic. CEO mindset.
Don't get lazy. When it comes to making money, you can't get lazy. I was in bed last night and I enjoyed my holiday. Guess what? Today isn't a holiday and neither is tomorrow. We must rest. You have to have a safe haven away from work. However, when it's time to work, you have to work. I want to make some extra money this summer because I want to.

I want you to join me. I've already started talking about it on Facebook and women are signing up. I want to work with hungry people. If you're not hungry, you'll never pick up the fork and dive into the work. Do you think you can sell 100 t-shirts in one month or 100 t-shirts in 3 months? Pick which one and read with your undivided attention.

1) You have to be willing to put in 4 weeks of work to flip the investment.
2) You have to have $100
3) You have to be willing to be a salesman and not be scared to sell to complete strangers
4) You have to submit all homework assignments on time or I'm going to drop you when I wake up the next morning (no jokes)

We start next Monday. 4 Live Classes that you will be able to access on my website. 4 Conference Calls every Sunday Night to do group think tanks and help one another reach our goals. I'll also be checking in via email if I catch you slipping in anyway or doing something that's not just right.

So...are you in?

If so, click here and get your seat. I'm pushing conversions right now in my Facebook Inbox and I haven't even started on Instagram. I'm going to fill these 20 seats. Beat me to it and grab your seat. Seats close Friday Night.

T-Shirt Class Sales Announcement #2
Title: I Can't Believe This. We're Hitting $30K! #Surprise

I'm opening up more seats...
I woke up Tuesday with an idea and it's Friday and the first wave of #HustleSchool with our #SummerHustle class is about to be full. People are hungry for money this summer. That's a

fact. I'm including myself in this number. If you're scared, I want you to know that your fear is only linked to your current circumstance. We don't move because we are looking at what's around us. Here's the thing about money. Money comes to those that aren't scared to put themselves out there. I've got a confession to make. After bible study this past Wednesday, I went out with a friend and did karaoke for the FIRST TIME in my entire life. No one went up with me. It was just me in front of an entire restaurant and I only knew one person.

I chose a song and went into the bathroom. I listened to the song for a few seconds and then proceeded back into the restaurant. I waited until the dj called my name and I went up. I grabbed the mic and began singing.

Now I can get up and teach in front of strangers about God but singing Until the End of Time by Justin Timberlake and Beyonce is different. Completely different. What's the point of me telling you this?

I did the karaoke on purpose. I wanted to prove to myself that I could do something I've always watched others do.

This T-Shirt biz class beginning next Monday isn't just for those with t-shirts. Some who have signed up are using this for future reference to help them sell whatever they desire. This is an e-commerce class at the end of the day. I want you to get away from fear and jump into faith.

I've extended the amount of seats to 30. That's going to be $30,000 earning potential with all of us combined. I don't know what you could do with $1K but it's up to you. I'm going to teach you how to get it and you'll hustle to make it reality. Seats close tonight at midnight.

Are you ready? If so, click here and get your seat.

-Genesis

Online Course/Class Sale
Title: How You Can Turn $20 into $500 in 30 Days! #ListenUp

I was up until 7 am this morning…

(Insert Name), I know that this sounds like it is in reverse but it is true. I didn't go to bed until the sun came up because I was working on something so exciting that I couldn't stop until it was finished.

It's my #LevelUp Webinar that I turned into an e-course and it's only $20! It's a 5 Course module meant to get you to start taking real courses of action today! Literally!

Each module includes courses of action for you to take and implement. Many of you need to clear out the clutter in your life and just focus on building your business. If you decide to put it off will you be a dollar richer? What will happen if you decide to invest in my course? You will make more than $20. After testing these modules on previous clients, the average first month was $1000-$3000 for the first 30 days. Now I know you can at least make $500 this month.

Have you seen someone out there selling things that aren't even half as good as what you know you can do and they are making money? So what's your excuse with your gifted and anointed self?

This e-course is not for those who have decided to be a benchwarmer. I'm looking to equip those who are ready to get into the game! By utilizing these tips and tricks, you will start selling within 30 days. You will learn how to close deals and have your bank account singing. Most importantly, you will be operating in purpose and will have the opportunity to bless somebody else after growing your business during the next 30 days.

Click here to get your seat. Registration closes at midnight tonight.

Want the full package plus learn about clarity for branding, product development, e-course creation, social media strategy, and more?

Then the Addicted to Purpose Class is perfect for you. This class begins on December second. Seats are available for this class and you will receive your Addicted to Purpose Welcome Kit afer signing up! Click here to learn more!

Hope to see you in class soon!
Love,
Genesis Dorsey

WEBSITES & PLATFORMS & TOOLS

PRINT & DESIGN & VIDEO

- **Print**
  - Paper Printing Needs
    - Vistaprint
    - Moo
    - Staples
    - FedEx
    - Overnight Prints
    - Packlane (Custom Boxes)
  - Signage
    - StickersBanners
    - Build A Sign
    - Display It At Church
  - Self-Publishing Books
    - Createspace (Amazon)
    - Ingram Spark
    - Blurb
    - Lulu
    - 48 Hour Books
  - Bulk Print Items
    - DiscountMugs
    - 4Imprint
    - 24 Hour Wristbands
    - Allied Shirts (Clothing)
  - Dropshipping Clothing
    - Printful

- Print Aura
- Printify
- Spreadshirt
- Merchify
- **Design**
  - Adobe Creative Suite
  - Canva
  - Pixelmator for Mac
  - PicMonkey
  - Over (app for phone)
- **Design Tools/Resources**
  - Creative Market
  - Envato
  - Pixeden (Mockups)
  - Covervault (Book Mockups)
  - Etsy (Clipart, Themes, ect.)
  - Pinterest (Design Inspiration)
  - Mockupworld (Mockups)
- **Photography**
  - Death to Stock Photo
  - Pixabay
  - Unsplash
  - KaboomPics
  - nappy.co
  - Create Her Stock
  - CreationSwap
  - Burst (Shopify)

- Pixels
- PicJumbo
- Styled Stock
- **Video**
  - Final Cut Pro
  - iMovie
  - Biteable
  - Apps
    - Quik
    - InShot
    - OBS Studio
    - Switcher Studio
    - Stream Monkey

COMMUNITY BUILDING TOOLS

- **All-In-One**
  - Ontraport
  - Infusionsoft
  - Hubspot
- **Email Marketing**
  - Mailchimp
  - Mailerlite
  - ConvertKit
  - AWeber
  - Constant Contact
  - Benchmark
  - Emma
  - Drip
  - Campaign Monitor

- **Email Marketing Plugins**
  - Privy
  - SumoMe
  - MailMunch
- **Website Platforms**
  - Squarespace
  - Wordpress
  - Weebly
  - Wix
  - E-Commerce
    - Shopify
    - Ecwid
    - BigCartel
    - Square
    - BigCommerce
    - WooCommerce

Online Courses
- Teachable
- Thinkific
- Udemy

Membership Portals
- Self-hosted through your site
- Memberspace

- Mighty Network
- Paid Memberships Pro (Wordpress)
- Member Mouse (Wordpress)
- Ontraport (all-in-one-system)

Landing Pages
- Leadpages
- Unbounce
- Instapage

Text-to-Join Companies
- Textiful
- Easy Texting
- Simple Texting

Domains & Hosting
- GoDaddy
- Google
- NameCheap

Website Hosting (for Wordpress & Custom Built Sites)
- DreamHost
- BlueHost
- GoDaddy

Purchasing Themes for Wordpress/Blogger
- Elegant Themes
- ThemeForest
- Creative Market
- Etsy
- Female Focused Themes

- Blue Chic
- A Prettier Web
- Pretty Darn Cute

Wordpress Plugins

- WooCommerce
- Yoast SEO
- Paid Memberships Pro
- Bloom by Elegant Themes
- Ninja Forms
- WordFence
- Seriously Simple Podcasting

STRATEGY & MONEY RESOURCES

Team Management

- Glip
- Basecamp
- Asana
- Slack

Financial Planning

- LivePlan
- InDinero

Payment Gateways & Billing

- PayPal
- Stripe
- Square
- authorize.net
- bill.com

Payment Tools

- SamCart
- ThriveCart
- Moonclerk

Accounting & Book Keeping & Payroll

- Wave
- Quickbooks
- Freshbooks
- Bench
- ADP Payroll
- Sure Payroll

SMALL BUSINESS RESOURCES

Business Setup
- Small Business Association (SBA) (sba.gov)

Business Networking & Mentorship
- SCORE (score.org)
- Local Chamber of Commerce
- meetups.com
- Eventbrite
- Linkedin
- Check Local Library for Classes & Events

Resources List from SCORE

American FactFinder: Census information on the demographics of your community including population, housing and the economy

Business USA: A centralized, one-stop platform for businesses to access services to grow and hire

Federal Business Opportunities (FedBizOpps): A database of federal government contracting opportunities

IRS Small Business Portal: Answers to small business tax questions, plus access to forms and publications, a video library, an event calendar and other online tools and products

Minority Business Development Agency (MBDA): Supports businesses in minority communities by providing grant and loan information, business opportunities and business certification resources

National Association for the Self-Employed: Nonprofit membership association representing the small business community in Washington, DC

National Business Association: Group buying association provides its members with support programs, useful products and services and business-building resource materials

National Federation of Independent Businesses (NFIB): Nonprofit association representing small and independent businesses

National Women's Business Council (NWBC): Provides independent advice and policy recommendations to the President, Congress, and the US Small Business Administration on economic issues important to female business owners

SCORE: SCORE, "Counselors to America's Small Business," is an SBA resource partner, dedicated to entrepreneur education. SCORE has over 12,000 volunteers with years of business experience available to help small business owners through on-on-one counseling, business tools and training programs

Small Business Administration (SBA): District offices in all 50 states provide resources, training and specialists to help start and grow businesses

Small Business Development Centers (SBDCs): Resources vary by location, but typically include things like assistance with business planning, access to financing, counseling services and classes

Small Business Legislative Council: A coalition of trade and professional associations

Social Security Online: Help for employers

US Chamber of Commerce Small Business Nation: Membership is dominated by small businesses with 100 employees or less. The Chamber's website has resources, toolkits on a variety of business topics and information on how you can get your voice heard in Washington, DC.

US Department of Commerce Department: Comprised of 12 different agencies, the Department promotes job creation and economic growth and works to strengthen America's position in the global marketplace.

US Department of Labor Bureau of Labor Statistics: Information on U.S. working conditions, labor market activity, and price changes in the economy

US Export Assistance Center (USEACs) Export.gov offers information about export assistance programs and services.

US Patent and Trademark Office: Grants U.S. patents and registers trademarks

Women's Business Centers (WBCs): Education centers for women business owners

Women's Business Enterprise National Council (WBENC): Provides assistance and education to certified women's business enterprises (WBEs) and government entities

Franchising
- International Franchise Association (IFA)
- The Franchise King
- Franchising.com
- FranChoice
- FranNet

Home-Based Business
- Working Naked
- My Own Business
- Home Business Magazine

Legal Information and Documents

- Company Corporation
- LegalZoom
- Nolo
- RocketLawyer

Small Business Magazines

- Entrepreneur
- Fast Company
- Inc.
- Smart Hustle
- Success Magazine

Small Business Websites

- AllBusiness
- Bloomberg Business
- Forbes
- Huffington Post: Small Business
- SmallBizDaily
- Small Business Trends
- Startup Nation
- Startup Professionals
- Wall Street Journal: Small Business

CHURCH SPECIFIC TOOLS

Church Management Systems

- Breeze
- Church Community Builder
- Fellowship One

Giving Tools

- Givelify
- tithe.ly
- PushPay
- MoGiv

Church Creative Tools

- ProChurch Studio
- LiveSwap from CreationSwap
- Pop Signs

Free Church Design Resources

- open.life.church
- https://newspringnetwork.com/resources
- https://seeds.churchonthemove.com/resources
- http://pixelpreacher.net/freebies/
- https://nlccreative.squarespace.com/

Church Blogs/Resources

- prochurchtools.com
- catalystleader.com
- churchleaders.com
- https://www.life.church/leadershippodcast/

SOCIAL MEDIA TOOLS

Designing

- Canva
- Wordswag (iPhone app)
- Adobe Photoshop
- Pixelmator for MAC

Scheduling

- Buffer
- Hootsuite
- CoSchedule
- Meet Edgar
- Planoly (Instagram)
- Later (Instagram)
- Grum (Instagram)

Maintenance

- Facebook Business Manager
- Facebook Pages App for Phone

Additional Tools

- LinkTree
- FameBit (for influencers & creators)
- MSGHero
- BuzzSumo
- Bitty
- Adobe Spark

GOOD ARTICLES/RESOURCES

Social Media Blogs
- Social Media Examiner
- Agora Pulse
- Socially Sorted
- Buffer Blog
- Sue B. Zimmerman

Facebook Ads
- Facebook Blueprint Courses
- https://moz.com/blog/10-things-ive-learned-while-learning-facebook-ads
- https://blog.bufferapp.com/facebook-ads

Podcasts
- How I Built This
- Masters of Scale
- TEDTalks Business
- Shopify Masters
- Side Hustle School
- EntreLeadership Podcast
- The Church Leaders Podcast
- ProChurch Podcast
- New Churches Q&A

Books

- How to Win Friends & Influence People by Dale Carnegie
- The 7 Habits of Highly Effective People by Stephen Covey
- It by Craig Groeschel
- How to Lead Like Jesus by Ken Blanchard
- Zero to One by Peter Thiel and Blake Masters
- Purple Cow by Seth Godin
- Crushing It by Gary Vaynerchuk
- Rich Dad, Poor Dad by Robert T. Kiyosaki
- The 4-Hour Workweek by Timothy Ferriss
- The ONE Thing by Gary Keller and Jay Papasan
- Soar by TD Jakes
- Hooked: How to Build Habit-Forming Products by Nir Eyal, Ryan Hoover
- Think and Grow Rich by Napoleon Hill
- Growth Hacker Marketing: by Ryan Holiday
- Contagious: Why Things Catch On by Jonah Berger

NOTES/IDEAS/BRAINSTORM AREA

_____

_____

_____

_____

_____

_____

_____

_____

_____

NOTES/IDEAS/BRAINSTORM AREA

_____

_____

_____

_____

_____

_____

_____

_____

_____

NOTES/IDEAS/BRAINSTORM AREA

_____

_____

_____

_____

_____

_____

_____

_____

_____

NOTES/IDEAS/BRAINSTORM AREA

_____

_____

_____

_____

_____

_____

_____

_____

_____

_____

NOTES/IDEAS/BRAINSTORM AREA

_____

_____

_____

_____

_____

_____

_____

_____

_____

NOTES/IDEAS/BRAINSTORM AREA

NOTES/IDEAS/BRAINSTORM AREA

_____

_____

_____

_____

_____

_____

_____

_____

_____